The Indie Writer's Handbook

AF271422

Designed for Independentl,
Published Authors

By: David Wind

<><><>

How to be a Professional Writer and
Survive Outside the
Traditional Publishing World.

DAVID WIND

If you are looking for information on:

How To Write a Best Seller

<>

How To Find an Agent

<>

How To Find a Traditional Publisher

<>

How To Sell Tens of Thousands of Your Books Daily

<>

How To Market Your Books and Make a Fortune

<>

THIS HANDBOOK IS NOT FOR YOU!

If you are looking for information on being, or becoming an independently published professional writer:

THIS HANDBOOK IS FOR YOU!

The Indie Writer's Handbook

Designed for Independently Published Authors

By: David Wind

<><><>

How to be a Professional Writer and Survive Outside the Traditional Publishing World.

ColSaw Publications
© by David Wind, 2019
ISBN-13: 978-1-7339495-2-1
ISBN-10: 1-7339495-2-6
Cover: *Steven Novak*
Editing: *Lacie Redding*

DAVID WIND

TABLE OF CONTENTS

Contents

DEDICATION

To those writers whose imagination turns into stories and whose stories enthrall their readers.

Are you one?

"For your born writer, nothing is so healing as the realization that he has come upon the right word."—Catherine Drinker Bowen

"Don't tell me the moon is shining; show me the glint of light on broken glass."— Anton Chekhov

"And by the way, everything in life is writable about if you have the outgoing guts to do it, and the imagination to improvise. The worst enemy to creativity is self-doubt."— Sylvia Plath

DAVID WIND

Dear Reader,

After much discussion with my editor, and at certain points within this handbook, we have taken a slight variation from traditional editing principles in the discussions of Independent publishing and Traditional publishing. This variation, or detour if you will, is used to highlight the differences and similarities between Independent (Indie) publishing and Traditional publishing by the use of capitalization.

David Wind

THE INDIE WRITER'S HANDBOOK

A Special Forward
From Mel Jolly

Hey, friend!

So you wrote a book or you're writing a book. Either way, congratulations! That's no small task and if you're picking up *The Indie Writer's Handbook*, you must be thinking about what's next for your career and for that book you so painstakingly crafted.

When David first approached me to write this forward, I thought, "Who? Me?" Then I remembered, "Oh right. I've been working in the publishing industry for 10 years." That's not as long as David has been writing books, but it's long enough for me to have witnessed the birth of Indie publishing as we know it and watch it go through the ups, downs, and growing pains it took to become the booming industry it is today.

If you want to reach readers (and I'm guessing you do... and probably a lot of them), the number one thing you need is to know without a shadow of a doubt is that your book is going to help people.

Say what now?

Yes, really. I don't care what kind of manuscript you've written, books make people's lives better.

Maybe you wrote a thrilling mystery that will give your reader a desperately needed escape from reality. Or maybe you lovingly crafted an adventurous romance that will take your reader on a whirlwind adventure through the streets of London. Or maybe you built a non-fiction tome filled with advice on how to help the reader get over their fears just like you did.

Whatever you've created, thank you. The world needs your words. And the world needs to receive your book in the best shape possible. When you are a published author, you are so much more than that. You are an entrepreneur and small business owner. You are the CEO and the CFO and the Creative Director and Marketing Director... Oh the power! And with great power comes great responsibility and So. Many. Decisions.

It can be easy to get overwhelmed. After years of fighting overwhelm and teaching others to do it too, here's one simple tip I can offer you. Look at the unknown. Stare straight at the scary thing and arm yourself with knowledge so you can make smart decisions.

If you want people to read (and hello... pay for!) your book, you need to give that book baby of yours the best possible shot in this over stimulated, overwhelmed, and busy world. This means you've got to create an irresistible product that practically sells itself.

What would it be like if the producer of your favorite TV show was like... "Don't worry, guys! We can fire the design team. Imma just take a cast pic with my phone and send it to Netflix. Everyone hold still."

Would you have ever started watching *Stranger Things*?

What if there was zero editing and you had to watch every scene where the actor said the wrong line or you could see the boom mic at the top of the frame?

No?

Books are the same way. You have some decisions ahead of you, but you already did the hardest part. You created something from nothing! (Dang. That's pretty amazing when you think about it.)

Now you can use *The Indie Writer's Handbook* to arm yourself with the knowledge you need to be a smart, savvy, and professional author and get your book into the world! The answers are here. What you do with them is up to you.

—Mel Jolly,
meljolly.com

[Publisher's Note: [Mel Jolly, Author Consultant, Project Manager, and Assistant for multiple NYT and USA Today Bestselling authors, has been "Keeping Authors Out of the Loony Bin Since 2009."]

THE INDIE WRITER'S HANDBOOK

INTRODUCTION

Welcome to the World of Independent Publishing.

But don't expect to read a normal how-to book; it's more of a one-sided conversational type of book. Well, perhaps I should say it's more of a one-sided conversation on my end—consider it a mentoring of sorts, but you are more than welcome to join in.

Also, in the interest of disclosures, this is not one of those *I'm going to teach you how to make lots of money if you buy my program books*. I don't have a program. There is nothing in the guide for you to buy from me, nor are there any associate or sales links where I make commissions from links to other things—but I'll admit it would be nice if you buy my novels. :-)

From this point on, the word we'll use for describing the type of writer/author you are choosing to be, is '***Indie***'. Prior to publishing your first book, fiction, or non-fiction, you are a 'writer'. Once you've published your first non-fiction book, short story, or novel, you officially become an 'author'—in this case, an Indie author. I believe writers write; and authors promote. And yes, you can be a writer and an author at the same time.

If you are a traditionally published author who has decided to publish an Indie book, or you are publishing your backlist, then you become a '***Hybrid***' author: one who works in both publishing landscapes.

I have been asked, over and over, "What's the difference between being an 'Indie' author and a Traditional author?"

In its simplest form, a Traditional author is a writer who has been published by a traditional publishing house (Putnam, Simon & Shuster, to name two); while, an Indie writer is both writer and publisher.

Although both writers do the same job and go through the same publishing processes, the differences within the publishing processes are significant, which is why this handbook has been developed. This book should not be looked at as a bible-like instrument of the rules of publishing; it is more a guide of suggestions and ideas, backed by experience, to help with the publishing aspects of an Indie writer/author/publisher, and designed to help keep everyone on a professional level.

Before we begin in earnest, you should know certain important basics:

Who is David Wind?

I am a *hybrid* author; of the 40 novels I've published, more than half have been traditionally published through Simon & Schuster, Dell, Dutton, Pinnacle, Worldwide, and others. I traditionally published my first book in 1981, and in 2008 I became an Independently published writer, author, and publisher. In the years since becoming an Indie, I have gained much experience, which has taught me how the differences between Traditional and Indie Publishing are easily shown; yet these differences can be difficult to overcome.

As to my writing credentials: I am an Indie *Hybrid* Author, a member of The Author's Guild, The Mystery Writers of America, SFWA (Science Fiction & Fantasy Writers of America), Novelists, Inc., an original member of the Romance Writers of America, ALLi (Alliance of Independent Authors), and am currently the Vice President of the Florida Chapter of the Mystery Writers of America. My full bio can be found at the back of this handbook.

What Is Indie Publishing?

Today's version of independent publishing has changed from the origins of what traditional publishing considered independent publishing to be. The original concept was to create a sector of publishing made up of small press publishers not aligned with the big traditional publishing houses. In other words, these publishers were independent of traditional publishing houses and therefore Independent publishers. These publishers brought out fiction novels and non-fiction books, not so much as to be in direct competition with the big publishing companies, but to create a place catering to readers who sought works outside the mainstream—a place where readers can discover new writers.

Before I get into contemporary Indie/self-publishing, a bit of history is called for. And our history has taught us, contrary to popular (Traditional) thinking, self-publishing is an integral part of our history.

Yes, I said integral. Think about some of the most famous, most literate, and most important writers of their time and ours, and you will find the list of self-published writers to be significant. L. Frank Baum, Edger Allen Poe, Mark Twain, and even William Strunk, Jr. self-published during their lives as writers. There are more, but I do believe I've made my point.

There was and is also self-publishing in the twentieth and twenty-first centuries, which well into the first decade of 2000, was considered vanity publishing ... a publishing no-no for a professional writer. Then along came Amazon, bringing with it a new meaning to the phrase *Independent Publishing.* This version of self-publishing, known as Print-On-Demand publishing, started the Indie writer revolution. Soon thereafter, the eBook industry was born. People who had always dreamed of writing flooded the gates of Amazon, and few of the early comers to the industry did extraordinarily well. This new method of publishing novels, non-fiction, and electronic books became known as Independent Publishing, and developed into a large part of the publishing and book-selling world. Amazon was followed by Barnes & Noble and Apple's iBooks, Kobo then joined in the fray.

These new Independent publishers gave the power of publishing to the authors themselves. In the beginning of this twenty-first century publishing revolution, Amazon empowered writers. And as the eBook phenomenon grew, a new generation of best-selling authors was created by the use of this new and powerful publishing tool. These self-published authors—many of whom were both traditionally published and self-published—called themselves Indie Writers, Indie Authors, Hybrid Authors, and Indie publishers.

After the first few years of massive growth and sales, rivaling the giant brick and mortar publishers, reality struck. Readers turned selective, becoming more and more careful about the Indie books they selected, in spite of the enticement of lower prices for eBooks.

It became evident this reader selectivity was directly caused by the avalanche of books released by droves of the new Indie writers. These writers were producing far too many of their books, doing it quickly, and unprofessionally. There were far too many sub-par works being offered to the reading public. Poor writing, poor editing, subpar quality self-made covers, and an overall unprofessionalism conspired to give the reading public extraordinarily poor products.

A change was needed, and it was coming.

A Brief History of Self-Publishing

You may or may not have heard this: I have. Many times. "Self-published writers using vanity presses are inferior writers who self-publish because their work isn't good enough for traditional publishers."

This is a long-held view of many traditional publishing house staffers and writers, who believe if they haven't selected you for publishing, then the work isn't good enough to be published. Well, I don't hold with that belief. I believe if a writer maintains their work on a professional level, it is up to the reading public to judge the writer by their own reading standards and the book's merits.

What exactly is vanity publishing, as opposed to indie publishing?

Before we acquired the ability to become independently published authors, vanity publishing was the only other method available. The name, *Vanity Publishing*, was created to describe those people who were absolutely determined to publish a book, usually memoirs, autobiographies, and biographies; however, novels were vanity published as well. The quality of the writing of most of these self-published books made absolutely no difference to the companies (usually referred to as vanity presses) publishing the books.

Thus, the reputation for vanity and/or self-published books was poor, and readers along with publishing professionals, began to equate self-publishing as vanity publishing.

While most vanity-published writers were not very good at their craft, the predatory publishers of vanity books were exceptionally good at their jobs, which was not to bring out a creditable, and well-crafted piece of work; rather, it was to deceive people and make money. A lot of money! Vanity publishers were (and still are) more predator than publisher. I have listened to horror stories of people spending upward of six thousand dollars or more to have their hardcover books printed, most of which are still in their garages.

Then came one of the most innovative happenings in contemporary publishing. POD (Print On Demand) was born. Suddenly, paperback novels, non-fiction works, and eBooks became a viable publishing option for writers. It was at this juncture—when Print On Demand was first brought out by Amazon's CreateSpace and a few others such as Lucy—the Indie publishing era was born. Within months it was an industry!

At this time the two types of publishing, vanity and Independent, seemed to morph together in the minds of most traditional publishing professionals; and, the same blending occurred to many in the reading public. All believed anyone who self-publishes has brought out a vanity book.

Let's try to set the record straight: In today's publishing world, and for most of us who are Indie writers, vanity publishing is not what we do! Professional Indie authors are just that, professionals. We Indie authors, just like traditional authors, have those who are good at their craft, and those who are not. What makes an even bigger difference between good and not good, is professionalism. A professional writer not only knows what is needed to make their books work, they use the tools of the profession to make sure of it, from the use of writing software to human editors and artists.

With those thoughts in mind, this guide has been created to help those entering the Indie publishing field to learn what it means to write and publish professionally; and, to help the new Hybrid authors to continue as both Indie and Traditional professionals. But more specifically, to help anyone involved in Indie publishing.

For traditionally published authors, the creative process basically ends with the final submission of the manuscript, with exceptions for specifically requested editorial rewrites. Once turned in, the manuscript goes through the full publication process. This process can take from (depending on the book, its contents, and its publishers) six months to two years—although under a year is extremely rare with the exceptions of whistle blower or tell-all books of current happenings. While the author is kept in the loop to a degree, the traditional publisher's staff handles the publishing process from editing, to cover design, to marketing and advertising, and finally to distribution.

When the Indie author's manuscript is completed, the Indie writer does not stop there. They now handle the publishing process, which, for the Indie writer, is an entirely creative process. The reality of what this means can be summed up this way: An Indie writer is responsible for every aspect of the book they have written and will be publishing. This responsibility must be handled in the same manner as if a traditional publishing house was publishing the book.

Beginning with Chapter 1, Step 1, this handbook has been designed to walk you through the publishing steps needed to produce a professionally crafted and published book, fiction, or non-fiction.

While the publishing process is perhaps the biggest difference between the traditional and independent writer, it is also the largest creative difference; Indie publishing allows the writer to control the entire publishing process for their work. If you are a 'newbie' this statement may not strike you as powerful ... yet. Trust me, it will one day.

In the following pages, we will also cover, step by step, the basics of getting your book into the hands of your readers, starting from the time you finish your final draft until the day your book appears on the virtual bookshelf, the brick & mortar bookshelf, or both.

What this handbook will not tell you, is how to sell thousands of books before you wake each morning, or how to make a million dollars with your books; rather, it explains how to create a professionally published book or novel to compete within its market genre.

Above it all, and redundantly, the purpose of this handbook is to guide you through the process which begins when you have completed your manuscript and you consider yourself ready to introduce this new work to the world—and as an Indie author/publisher, this handbook will help you to create a **professionally** published book.

A Word of Caution

Understand, if you are planning to be an Indie writer/author, and want to earn enough royalties to enable you to have a professional writing career and pay your publishing expenses, you must meet the same standards traditional publishers require of their authors and of their products: a well written story; professional editing, copy editing, and proofreading; a professional cover; correct and current legal copyright and ISBN filings; and, solid marketing. Once you've done all the basic steps, you have a chance of becoming successful.

Those of you who are traditionally published, and who may or may not publish independently, are discovering the traditional publishers are now requiring you to do much of the same marketing work as Indie writers do to be successful—full social media, BookBub marketing, Twitter, and much more. *Or Have they offered you **more** of a royalty share for doing their work?*

Now, if you're ready, turn the page.

.

THE INDIE WRITER'S HANDBOOK

CHAPTER 1
STEP 1
The Final Draft—Or Is It?

Your book is done, you stare at the last words on the last page and there is a sensation of triumph like nothing you've ever felt before. Writing a book is no small accomplishment. Then reality hits. *How do I get it into readers' hands?* Once your book (non-fiction/fiction) is written, you need to start the first of the ten basic steps in the Indie publishing process. *How to get your work into a reader's hands is not one of those steps.* However, it is the very beginning of the final pre-publication processes. Rest assured, when you are really ready, you'll have your answer, for now, we'll go in order of the steps.

There are ten basic steps in the initial publishing process, which are followed by another eight pre/post publishing steps. Once steps 1-9 of the initial publishing process are completed, such as the editing steps, cover design, copyrighting and others, your next steps (10 & 11) are to set up the publishing and selling outlets, and send your book to the beta readers, which is the very first time your book reaches a reader's hands.

Steps in the Publishing Process
1. Final manuscript draft
2. Formatting for editing purposes
3. Editing
    a. Structural Editing
    b. Line Editing
    c. Copy Editing
    d. Proof Reading
4. Cover Artist
5. Formatting for eBook and online sale
6. Formatting for Print Book sales online and bookstores
7. ISBNs
    a. ISBN for an eBook

STEP 1: THE FINAL DRAFT

A final draft generally comes after one or more rewrites. For me, my final draft—the one going to my editor—is usually my third draft (which is a combination of my second and third drafts). My second draft is done by working with the hard copy, rather than the electronic version.

After making all the corrections and changes by hand, I then work with the electronic version of the manuscript and make those changes on the computer. This also gives me the opportunity to consider and reconsider my handwritten changes.

Once that's done, I'll reread the manuscript to make certain it's what I want. Then, and only then, do I start the editing process. **Not *my* editing, my *editor's* editing**.

Without the proper editing, your book doesn't have the chance you need to make everything right. A good professional editor, an expert in the editorial process, will not only spot what's wrong but will spot what doesn't work from their trained perspective. Remember, you are extremely close to your work and in most cases, cannot be impartial.

Once the changes from the editor are implemented, it's time to move forward.

"But why do I need an editor? I know English, I'm a good writer, and I have great editing programs on my computer, like MS Word, or Grammarly, so why would I spend money on an editor?"

All I can do is ask you to think about this. Why do publishers pay editors to edit books? Why does every book, fiction, and non-fiction, go through the editing process at a traditional publishing house?

The answers are simple. A good editor does exactly what is necessary to make a book not just readable, but exceptional. Professional editing will make or break a book, and a book, no matter how good it is, cannot survive without proper editing,

One reason why so many Indie books are not given proper respect, is because many are of poor quality. Great stories tumble to the bottom of the pile, or are returned to the seller because of typos, misused words, and poor formatting. These issues are some of the reasons why you need a good editor to make certain your book not only rises above but presents your reader with an experience that gives them a reason to read more of your books. A professional editor can take a poorly written but exceptional story, and make it stand out. But if this great but poorly written story goes unedited by a professional, it will falter and...

In order to reach the editing step, you need to make sure your final draft is ready for editing. Editing is the first essential step to bring your book to the level of a professional writer and publisher. Nothing can substitute for good editing, and no writer can truly edit their own book for typos. The explanation for this stems from the fact that you are reading the words you wrote; and, since our mind already knows what the correct spelling is for the word we are reading, and by having this knowledge, our minds fill in incorrect spelling, missed letters, and basic typos with the correct ones. This is why you miss your own mistakes.

There are several types of editing; copy editing, line editing, and substantive editing. In most brick & mortar publishing houses, your main editor is your substantive editor. The most intensive form of editing is substantive editing, which involves working on and correcting the book's structure, organization, coherence, and logical consistency.

Once this is done, the editing process moves on to copy editing and line editing and then—

Now that we've gotten ahead of ourselves, let's draw back on the editing talk. Our next step is what I call pre-edit formatting. The purpose of which is two-fold.

First, it allows your manuscript to follow a specific style, as opposed to just writing. Second, if done properly, it will save you significant costs during the editing process. If an editor has to spend time adjusting the formatting so the editor can read easily and work better, it is time you pay for. Some editors work by word count, others by an hourly fee: either way, time is money.

So, please do pay attention to the next chapter, it's important for your book, your professionality, and your wallet.

CHAPTER TWO
STEP 2
Pre-Formatting for Editing

For Independent publishing, you have three publishing choices: Electronic; Print; or both. The two types are not mutually excludable but require different set-ups: formatting for publication will require two separately formatted manuscripts. For eBooks, there are also two distinct types of eBook software programming being used for eBooks. There are more types, but for the current standards, we will cover the two most important. To learn more about them, click here to go to makeuseof.com; Of course, there is also a minimum of two types of formatting for print books. Those depend on which publisher/distributer you will use to publish your print versions—but there are and will be even more versions of print formatting coming.

Most likely, as an Indie publisher you will use two print outlets: Amazon, for those books sold on Amazon, and another print distributor who offers Print On Demand (POD) for sales on non-Amazon sites and bookstores. I use Ingram Spark for anything not on Amazon.

Online publishers require specific formatting to be done for their platforms. These publishers, Amazon, Barnes & Noble, Apple, Kobo, and many others work in the two recognized standard programming categories of eBook formatting, either ePub or Mobi. Mobi is Amazon's exclusive programing and the only way Amazon publishes eBooks. Apple, Barnes & Noble, Kobo, and almost everyone else in the eBook industry publishes using ePub programming.

The type of formatting we will discuss at this point, is for your manuscript, not for the publishing process. Your manuscript needs to be set up properly for editing, so when the time comes for eBook formatting for publication, everything will already be in place.

Normally, once you have a style sheet, which is a file or form defining the layout of a document with such parameters as the line spacing, headings, margins, paragraphs and fonts, and use it for your manuscript, you will be able to start your next manuscript with the same style sheet, negating the need for pre-editorial formatting. A style sheet is also called a style set.

For our purposes, we will assume you have a completed book, which may or may not be formatted properly.

The way you format your manuscript depends on the program you use. There are a lot of programs designed specifically for manuscripts; however, I use MS Word, because (1) I find it the easiest and least demanding of the word processing programs; and, (2) when it comes to writing, I am a creature of habit. When GUI interfaces were introduced waaay back in history, I switched from WordPerfect, which was only in DOS to MS Word, and just kept going. I prefer not using online writing programs and websites: I don't like keeping my current work online when it's not necessary, but that's just the writer paranoia in me.

There are many programs available for Apple and PC machines for writing. Here are just a few, in no particular order:

- Microsoft Word – word processor, paid yearly;
- Scrivener – word processor, initial purchase/no annual fee;
- Google Docs – online word processor, free;
- yWriter – word processor, free;
- Hemingway App – style & grammar checker, free;
- Ulysses – word processer paid yearly;

Setting up your manuscript's basic formatting

Your basic style sheet will have many options. The most important basic options while creating your manuscript should be having your NORMAL settings ready to roll!

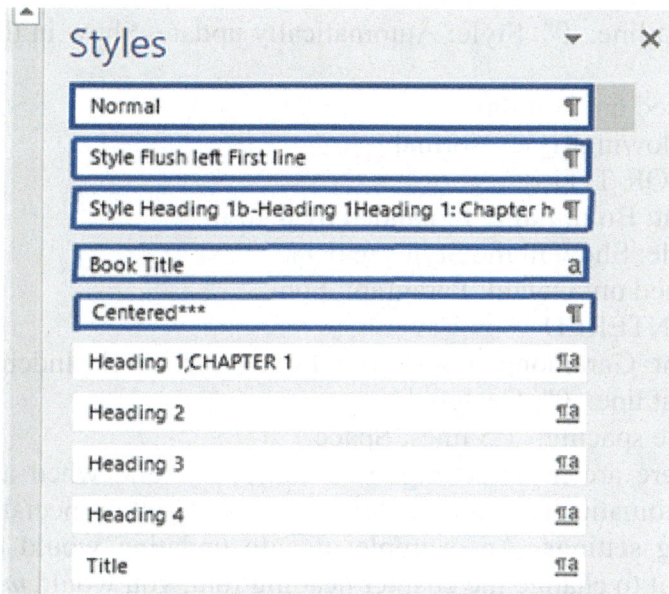

The top five settings shown in the graphic above are my base settings. I always keep my style sheet open during my writing—it's not necessary, just my own writing method.

You should work with the settings you're most comfortable using. As an example of the formatting set-up, here is the basic formatting behind my own settings.

NORMAL:

Font: (Default) Times New Roman, 12 pt, Indent

First line: 0.3", Left

Line spacing: 1.5 lines, Widow/Orphan control, Style: Show in the Styles gallery

CHAPTER HEADING:

Font: (Default) Garamond, 14 pt, Bold, Font color: Text 1, Indent

First line: 0", Centered, After: 6 pt.

No widow/orphan control, Level 1, Style: Linked, automatically update, Show in the Styles gallery

FIRST LINE FLUSH LEFT (I start my chapters this way)

Font: Bold, Indent

First line: 0", Style: Automatically update, Show in the Styles gallery

Based on: Normal

Following style: Normal

BOOK TITLE:

Font: Bold, Italic, Expanded by 0.25 pt.

Style: Show in the Styles gallery

Based on: Default Paragraph Font

CENTERED

Font: Garamond, 14 pt, Bold, Font color: Black, Indent

First line: 0", Centered

Line spacing: 1.5 lines, Space

There are more settings you can apply, and when activated, will automatically work within the manuscript, especially when updating settings. An example of auto updating would be when you want to change the chapter heading font, you would *modify* the chapter heading style, which would then update all chapter headings at the same time. The same can be done for the line spacing under Normal, etc. For those not familiar with style sheets, the normal setting is the setting for all body text within the manuscript.

The following graphics show the modification window for my style sheet's normal setting. Image (a) is the dialogue box showing the overall normal setting; image (b) is the underlying paragraph setting; image (c) is the underlying font setting.

NORMAL SETTING

Image a

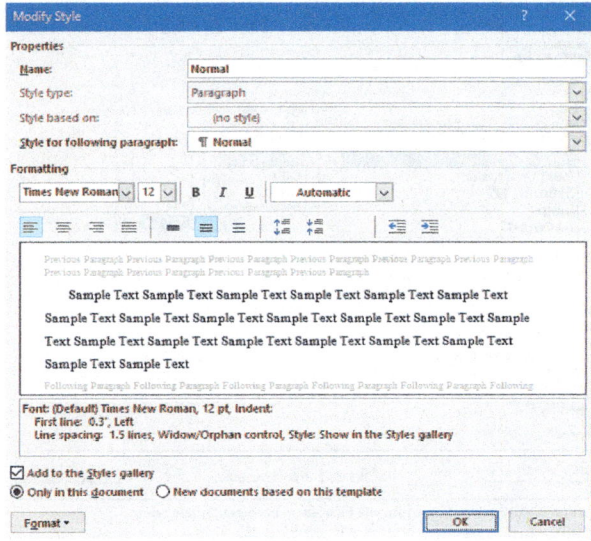

Image b

Image c

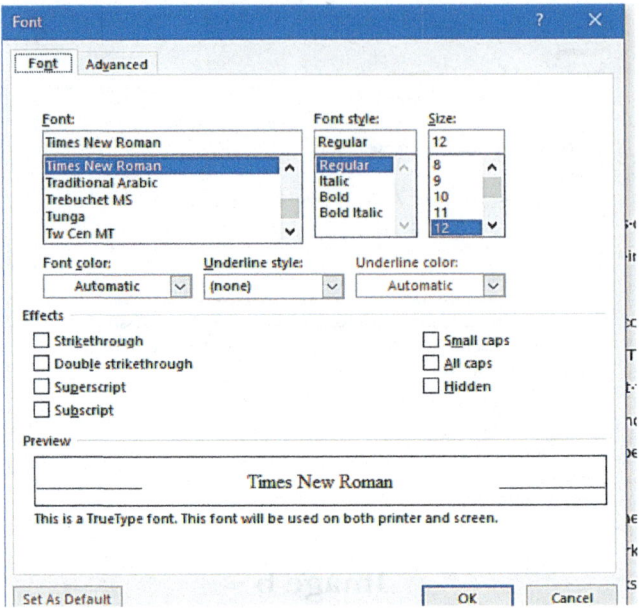

Image (d) the chapter heading modification window.
Image d

CHAPTER HEADING

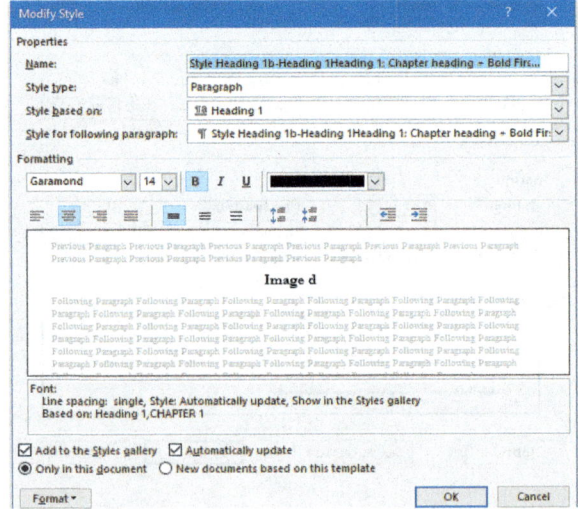

THE INDIE WRITER'S HANDBOOK

I format my manuscript to either 1.5 or double line spacing. The reason is so I can make editing changes or notes between the lines when I'm getting ready to do my third draft. Once done, professionally edited, and depending on length, I will change the line spacing to one of three settings: 1.5, 1.25 or 1.15.

For print books, you bear the printing costs, so the fewer pages, the less expensive the book is to produce and therefore a better price for your readers. The difference between 1.5 and 1.15 line spacing can, in some instances, amount to $1.50 per book in your printing costs.

At this point, having the proper pre-process formatting helps the editorial process move smoothly, and in turn it makes it much easier to reformat for either eBooks or print when you've reached that stage.

If you are really uncertain about formatting, or you prefer relegating the formatting, there are more formatting options than doing it yourself: using a professional formatting service, or a freelance formatter, when your manuscript is completed, is an option that works—the only downside is monetary, but time can be saved that way as well, and *time* as the saying goes, *is money*.

There are also highly qualified professional freelance editors who will format your book, usually for a slight additional cost over the editing charges. I will have a listing of services and vendors at the back of this handbook. But, remember, as the publisher, it is your job to contain expenses, and formatting isn't overly difficult to learn.

Once your manuscript is properly formatted, whether you format it yourself or use a professional formatter or service, then you have reached the point for the real editing process to begin.

While it seems you may need to use several professionals, that is not always the case. You can learn formatting. It is not difficult, especially if you consider what it takes to write a novel, or a non-fiction book. The editing is another story, and a professional editor should always be used, and you will soon see why.

[Click Here](#) for GCFLearnFree.org, an online free teaching website with lessons in setting up and using Style Sheets for MS Word.

I would also suggest you begin (if you haven't already) to familiarize yourself with the terms used in publishing. While there will be a resource section and a glossary included, the definitions below are important to know now.

~#~

There are definitions you'll need to know: Online Book Publisher; Online Book Retailer, and Aggregator.

Online Book Publishers

An online publishing company selling books it has published through its own retail store is categorized as an Online Book Publisher and eBook and print book retailer. Examples include Amazon's Kindle Direct Publishing (KDP) and KDP Print (POD), Apple's iBook store, Barnes & Noble's Press, and Kobo. Many of these companies form partnerships to distribute books to other retailers, e.g., KDP Print's Expanded Distribution program.

Online Book Retailers

An Online Book Retailer is a website company selling books but not publishing books and is categorized as an eBook and print book retailer. All of the companies listed in the above paragraph qualify for this category. There are also many vendors on the Internet who do not publish books but sell both eBooks and print books. These are your virtual bookstores.

Aggregator: A distributer of eBooks

Strictly speaking, an aggregator is an online distributer of eBooks. In reality, many aggregators not only distribute to their eBook partner online retailer sites like Apple, B & N, Kobo, and libraries; they offer their own retailing platform for eBooks. This does allow Indie writers to step outside the restraints of Amazon and offer their eBooks in wider distribution. Another aspect of an aggregator is they can distribute eBooks to channels where authors cannot submit directly. Scribd is an example of a subscription not accepting eBooks directly from authors. This also applies to getting your books into libraries, which aggregators offer to their authors.

CHAPTER THREE
STEP 3
Professional Editing

Editing can be broken down into four types or levels, which are, substantive editing; line editing; copy editing; and, proofreading.

THE EDITOR'S ROLE IN THE PUBLISHING
PROCESS

As a rule, the editor makes corrections, changes, and the necessary improvements to keep your manuscript consistent throughout. The editor makes sure your manuscript is at the level expected by its target audience. The overall purpose of the editing process is to manage the book's literary structure, including sentence structure, grammar, spelling, punctuation, and formatting.

The Difference Between the Editorial Processes of Traditional and Indie Publishing

Indie writing differs from Traditional publishing in several way. Most traditional publishers have an editor in charge of the book. This editor would be the *substantive editor*. In most cases, the substantive editor is also the line editor.

When the manuscript is delivered, the substantive editor, edits. Once the required rewrites (if such are necessary) are turned in, the editor does the final editing, hands it off to the copy editor, who may or may not be the proofreader as well. If not, the copy editor hands off the manuscript to the proofreader.

INDIE writers should hire either a substantive editor and a proofreader, or a single editor who does all editing jobs. It is important to understand that editing is not the expense to cut corners with, and it certainly isn't a do-it-yourself option, even if you graduated summa cum laude in English Lit. ***Why? Because you are too close to your work!***

As a traditional writer, once any requested revisions are in, it's the end of the road for you. The publisher takes it all over, usually including the cover. The next time you see the book is when you receive the galleys.

This is not so for the Indie writer. Once the editing process is completed—line editing, copy editing, and proofing—the manuscript is back in your hands. Your next responsibility as an Indie writer, is to re-read every word, line, and page to make sure you agree with the editing. If you don't, if you feel something doesn't work the way you believe it should, then you can do one of two things: change it yourself; or, discuss it with your editor and work it out. For the most part, your editor should be listened to. With some rare occurrences, you may overrule the editor, but this must be done only when it is a creative necessity for you, and not because of ego. Remember, your ego can hurt a book's chance to succeed.

When you've finished reading, making any further corrections you deem necessary, then it's time for additional proofreading. There should always be extra eyes on the words!

Personally, I hire a single editor for the line/copy/proofreading. When I receive the book back from my editor, I go through the book, page by page, making sure I'm in sync with the work the editor has done. If I'm unsure as to why something was done, I ask.

When I'm satisfied with what was done editorially, I go over the formatting and make any changes necessary for eBook conversion. Then, using the actual publishing platforms, I create a Mobi and/or ePub file. My next step is to send the file to two beta readers whom I trust. I have them read the book for content to let me know if I've done my job in suspending disbelief, if I've entertained them, if I've made them think, and if I did what I'd set out to do, create a novel for the reader to enjoy. I also ask my beta readers that as they read, to do additional proofreading. I know I ask a lot, yet, I've never had a beta reader look at me and say, "Seriously, you want all of that?"

If you ask me why I use a beta reader, I would tell you the driving factor in editing a manuscript for Indie writing and publishing is to understand how essential it is to know—no matter how careful you are, and no matter how great your editor is—misspellings, typos, misaligned formatting, and other errors can sneak past even the most accomplished of editors and proofreaders. This is the point where additional sets of eyes—at least two sets—are a huge benefit. Remember, you are an Indie writer, and you are carrying the baggage left behind by previous and poorly prepared Indie writers. You need to make the world know you are a professional. There are many more reasons to use beta readers, and one such is because beta readers can become your FANS!

With fans, come excellent reviews, and more sales, as your beta readers tell others they should read your books. View your beta readers as the foundation of your growing population of fans. Never mistreat them, and always keep in contact. It pays off in so many ways, including unexpected friendships.

Working With Your Editor:
The Stages of Editing for Indie Writers

As noted earlier, the main stages of editing are structural editing, line editing and copy editing. I consider proofreading as the fourth form of editing. *Structural editing* is also called *developmental editing*; and, some publishers also call *copy editing, proofreading*. As an Indie writer and publisher, I consider them separate, and so should you, if for no other reason than for the sake of your readers.

Manuscripts usually need several editorial passes. The time spent and the number of editing passes your editor will need to make will depend on your ability to self-edit before submitting. It also has to deal with your editor's working knowledge of your projected audience. It makes no difference how many editing passes it takes to bring your manuscript to be ready for publication, what is vital, is for the editing of your work to be done in a solid professional manner, which will ensure its readability.

STRUCTURAL EDITING / DEVELOPMENTAL EDITING

THE INDIE WRITER'S HANDBOOK

While Traditional publishers commonly consider the structural editor a developmental editor, that is not the usual case with Indie writers, as you are most likely submitting a finished manuscript rather than working with an initial outline the editor has guided you on. However, if you have a developmental relationship with your freelance editor, USE IT!

Again, depending on how deep your pockets are, you can hire a Structural Editor, a Copy Editor, and a Proofreader; however, if you are like me, and consider the entire cost of producing a book, when you find a single editor who handles your book like it was their own, I would hesitate to look further. As an average, most successful professional Indie writers I know use a single editor.

Once your editor begins work, they will do a read-through structural analysis. If they find problems at that stage, and if they are truly a professional, they will either send you back the manuscript with their suggested changes or discuss the changes with you. As an Indie writer, and as the publisher, it is up to you to act on the editor's suggestions. If you decide not to do what is suggested, then continue on with the process. If you decide to make the changes, do so and send the revised manuscript back to the editor.

LINE EDITING

Once the editor has completed the manuscript and any structural issues involving the story and storyline are corrected, the editor will do the full line editing. The purpose for line editing is to focus on your use of language, style, and to enable your writing to connect your story to your reader. Be very aware of what line editing is not: line editing it is not the search for errors in a line. Line editing scrutinizes the creative content, your style, and the language used to build sentences, paragraphs, and chapters.

Think of line editing as the most important aspect of the editing process, for it works to make certain your stylistic intention stays true to your story and your narration.

The website of a group of editors who have banded together to do freelance work, called the *New York Book Editors*, consider line editing to have the following features. (This list is only a few of the items line editors work on.)

- Extraneous sentences
- Overused words
- Run-on sentences
- Redundancies
- Tightening paragraphs
- Correcting confusing actions
- Unnatural phrasing
- Poor passages because of language
- Confusing narrative
- Improvement of pacing
- Words or phrases to enhance your meaning

COPY EDITING

What is Copy Editing?

The purpose of copy editing, unlike structural or line editing is to make sure your manuscript is "flawless". In traditional publishing, this is the last editorial step. As the copy editor is also a high-level proofreader, which is not necessarily so in the Indie world.

Copy editing corrects spelling, punctuation, grammar, and syntax. Copy editing deals with the internal consistency of the technical aspects of editing the manuscript: hyphenation, capitalization, numerals, and fonts. For non-fiction, a copy editor will check on factual statements.

When a copy editor checks for consistency within the manuscript, the editor is checking the consistency within the plot, the setting you've placed your characters in, and determining that those important little character traits that make your protagonist and antagonist become special, are both consistent and without discrepancies. There are a lot of ways to lose consistency. I can show you notes from my editor telling me exactly where one of my characters went from burgundy hair to blonde hair and back again. There was no mention of her coloring her hair. *Oooops!*

At times there tends to be some encroachment between the structural/line editor and the copy editor. This is usually because the line editor also checks for consistency. When a line editor sees a technical error, and although it's not their job to correct it. Rather, it's usually because line editors are so ah … driven (does that work or should I just say anal?), they tend to do so for the benefit of the manuscript.

It is important to remember the line editor and the copy editor are both responsible for the consistency of EVERYTHING in a manuscript, so there are always overlaps. Of course, as an Indie writer, if you are dealing with a single editor, there is no encroachment.

The one significant rule to be understood, is that copy editing/proofreading, should come only after the structural and line editing is completed.

In traditional publishing houses, copy editing / proofreading is the last step before production; with Independent publishing, it is usually a beta reader who ends up as your final proofreader.

While I believe, deeply, that an Indie writer must use a professional editor to ensure their final product is the most highly polished and the best it can possibly be, some of you either won't use an editor, or can't afford it. For those few of you who choose to go it alone, read the next paragraph, and memorize it. It may not make it into a second edition.

EDITING HACKS**

If you stubbornly insist on editing yourself, here are two hacks to help you in the editing process: The first, to protect your reader from typos, read your manuscript from cover to cover, **BACKWARDS,** one word at a time; and, the second hack is to either have someone read your manuscript aloud, to you, or if you write using MS Word, take advantage of the Read Aloud feature (control+ALT+space) and have Word read the manuscript to you.

DAVID WIND

**A 'hack' is now part of our daily lexicon, and instead of just
meaning to illegally break into a computer or a coded program, the word
has evolved to also mean a solution or work-around to a problem.*

CHAPTER FOUR
STEP 4
The Book Cover

Almost everyone, everywhere has heard the old cliché *A picture is worth a thousand words*. Not for you, amigo or amiga—not even close!

To you, the picture (hear the words 'book cover') can be worth tens of thousands of words. If you have an average length novel, say 75,000-100,000 words, that's what your cover is worth!

There are a lot of clichés and maxims talking about first impressions. Wait a sec … do you know why they call certain phrases clichés? It's because no matter how you try to phrase what you want to say, that particular phrase (cliché) is the best way to say a specific thing. So, without getting too far into those old sayings your parents, teachers, and grandparents loved to spout, let's use: *You can only make a first impression once*; and, just agree your book's cover is your first meeting 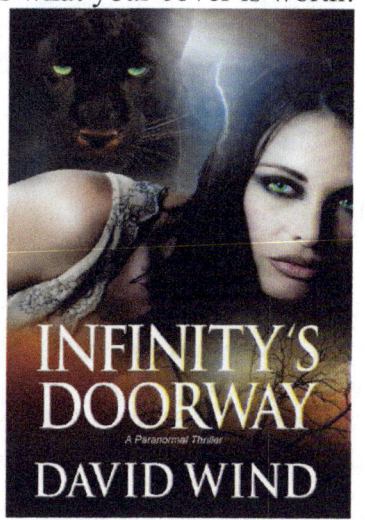 with your reader. As such, it is the single most important happening possible for you.

You have invested untold hours creating your book, or novel. You have even more time working to make it the best it can be. You invest money in the editing/formatting process, and as you prepare to publish, there is one important step yet to be taken, the cover. But then, like many of the early Indies published by amateur writers, you turn to an art program on your computer and dive headfirst into a cover creation. Your book sells ten copies in its first year, and you don't understand why.

Well, like editing, you're too close to the project, and your vision for a cover may not translate well to a potential reader, because you know what the book is about, they don't. The cover is the beginning of your selling synopsis—it must speak to the reader. And, unless you are a graphic artist of great repute, or an incredible artistic painter, leave it to a pro! Think of your cover as a tool for marketing what is behind it. Your cover is your salesperson! It's there on everyone's computer screen, cell phone, tablet, e-reading device, and on bookshelves of bookstores. You simply cannot get a more in-your-face salesperson than your book cover. But the cover needs to call to them, and that's not your job. Your job is to use words to entertain, and/or educate, and/or teach, or just tell your story.

The essential point of the lesson here is for you to understand your cover must communicate with the potential reader in a way similar to your words.

Hold on… For novels, there is something more to be said, and I hope one day this phrase will become a cliché.

"Covers are the window to your reader's imagination."

Understand, there is a real difference in the visual aspects of a cover between amateur work and professional work, especially when the professional is specifically a Book Cover Artist. Go on Amazon, or iBooks, or Kobo and browse… Then think about how the cover will look in a thumbnail of about one and a half inches wide. Can you do that and make it look not only visibly readable, but desirable as well? If you can, good for you. Most of us can't. Here's an example of one of my earliest eBook releases of a backlist novel with my homemade cover, which very shortly thereafter I realized wouldn't work, and I had a professional cover created.

The differences between the two are huge. The novel is a combination thriller and police procedural. The cover on the left has to do with *what I think* communicates with the reader. The cover on the right, was done by professional cover artist Steven Novak. When I look at it, I see a plane, and I see a man with a large gauge rifle standing on a runway. With my first glance I *feel* tension.

Tension is exactly what I wanted. I just don't have the technical ability to communicate to the reader with artwork, and I understand that, which is why I stopped on my first cover attempt and never do a cover myself.

Original Cover   Professional Cover Artist

Yes, you can save the cost of hiring a cover artist, usually from $150-$400 and more, depending on what you want for a cover, but using your own you could lose untold amounts of sales. If you want to be considered a professional writer and author, *use a pro, it is not a theory, it is a fact, and it works.*

Even when you have your cover done the right way, and over the period of a year, your sales do not reach what you believe they should, or what the books in your genre show for sales, and you've done all the right marketing, the option for an Indie writer to change the cover and make it more inviting is a practical and available option. For example, the two covers below show a change of cover.

This novel is the first in the series and has been downloaded over 65,000 times. (at the time of this writing) The cover was changed seven months before this writing. I experienced a ten percent increase in downloaded eBooks and a three percent increase in the print sales, and according to my sales figures, it has continued to hold at those levels.

Professional cover artists created the covers: both are excellent covers, but the cover on the right drew more eyes than the cover on the left. The cover artist followed my every wish for the cover on the left, the cover artist for the cover on the right heard what I had to say, and then created this. It wasn't what I expected, but it was exactly what I needed. And it was the perfect cover for my series.

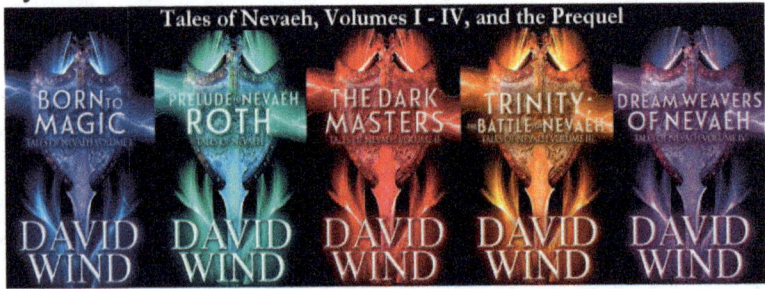

There are a lot of things you can do to make a cover great, including working with the cover artist on how you envision the book cover—but I encourage you to set your ego aside, just as you would for your editor, and listen to the artist—let the artist guide you. Even if it isn't the exact representation of what you thought you wanted, an experienced cover artist, one well versed in your genre, knows what types of covers sell. They also know what is allowed and what isn't by your retailers. You can also go to Amazon or Apple or any of the book-selling sites and take a peek at the "look inside" feature. See if the author gave the cover artist credit. If they did, then it's off to a new browser window to search out the artist on the Internet. Remember too, a professional cover artist can also set your covers to follow a specific pattern with your name and titles, which is how you build a brand for your work.

Of course, you'll give the artist a synopsis of your work, keep it concise, no more than two pages. If it's a novel, a non-fiction biography, or a true story type of book (like true crime), you should also include the protagonist and antagonist's descriptions. You can ask the artist to read the book or novel, but for most cover artists, you will pay their hourly fees while they read. Most good artists will get it right from a synopsis.

The Lower-Cost Professional Cover Option

There are many websites run by cover artists, and companies, producing high quality premade covers needing only your name and the title to be added, which is included in the cost shown for each cover. These covers are less expensive, ranging from as little as $25 and rising to $200. I have rarely seen or heard of much higher prices, and many artists charge about the same for a custom cover as the upper range of premade covers. The other issue you must check on, is to make certain the pre-made cover gives you the proper art copyright license so you are royalty-free for the artwork and will not be open for copyright infringement.

The way art royalties work, for us, is the professional cover artist (usually) pays for the specifically purchased stock art, and then passes their cost on to you, which leaves you royalty-free at that stage. There are exceptions, which the cover artist is obligated to tell you of, should the stock-art being purchased for your cover fall within certain boundaries, but that usually deals with the sales of books reaching into the hundreds of thousands.

eBook Covers

eBook covers are traditionally a flat cover for the product page on any of the sales sites, such as Amazon, Apple, etc. Some will allow a 3D version, but Apple specifically disallows 3D.

I do believe the flat offers a better overall view of the cover, but a 3D can be very eye catching. For myself, and many authors I know, we reserve the 3D for promotions and advertising, as the flat tends to stand as a more traditional way for professional authors to offer their books. That being said, as an Indie writer, the decision is always yours!

The 3D version along with the flat version, sometimes adds cost to the cover, as it usually includes a properly done spine as well as graphic manipulation.

But whether you use a flat version or 3D version, it must follow the rules and be the correct size, both in pixels (1800 x 2700) and in resolution (300 dpi).

Print Covers

The difference between eBook and print covers is very simple. Print covers have a front cover, a spine, and a back cover. Print covers will cost anywhere from fifty percent more to double the cost of an eBook cover, depending on the final design, the amount of text, and the artist's rates.

The artist can put in the ISBN and barcode on the back cover, if you supply them. But whoever you select to do your book printing and distribution (Amazon, IngramSpark, Draft2Digital, Barnes & Noble, etc.) will put your ISBN and the correct barcode on the back cover during the printing process. (ISBNs will be discussed in a later chapter.)

The take-away on book covers is, by having either a custom created cover or a professionally created pre-made cover, you will have a professional cover to enhance your novel and be your salesperson.

Remember, your book is competing in a huge world-wide marketplace and you want it to stand out and be noticed, which is a cover artist's job. Your job is to make the words inside the cover stand out.

I would like to close this chapter with an article on book covers from The Book Cover Designers. While I have mentioned several of the issues already, the article emphasizes what I have tried to pass on to you.

The Importance of Finding
The Right Cover For Your Book
And The Top 5 Mistakes Authors Make When
Choosing Book Covers*

Many readers claim they go by the popular saying that you shouldn't judge a book by its cover—either when they are browsing through tons of eBooks for their Kindles or when they are looking at paperback copies stashed on bookstore shelves. In both cases there will be judging.

One of the secrets to self-publishing a best-selling book is choosing a book cover that will pass the readers' judgmental test.

In the vast and exciting world of literature there are three types of book covers—bad covers, good covers, and great covers. And the right way to land a great cover for your book is to avoid some common, yet extremely overlooked mistakes every author is prone to making. Without further ado here, according to The Book Cover Designer*, are the top five mistakes you don't realize you're making when choosing your book cover.

1: GENERALIZATION

Nobody likes being called basic, plain, or common. You don't want your book to be seen as mediocre or passable, and generalization will definitely land you right there. Generalization is one of the worst mistakes you can make when choosing your cover art. Following the general stylization and atmosphere of the typical book covers in your preferred genre will not make your book stand out from the rest.

The key is to make your book break into your preferred literary genre—not to get lost in it.

You don't want your target audience to pass up your book because its cover fully blends in with the rest. You want your cover to catch the attention of the audience. You want your readers to come to a stop, to reach out and to buy your book. You want to break through the barrier of the generalization—not to get sucked into it. What makes a good break-through? Being catchy. But what makes a great break-through? Innovation.

2: NOT GETTING PERSONAL

Your book cover should speak to you. You'll probably ask *why should it speak to me personally and not to my audience?* It's simple. Your book is your own work of art. Your readers aren't just picking up some eBook, paperback, or hardcover. They are picking up a part of you. Your book represents you as an author; your work and artistry. The cover also represents the book in significant ways, which is why the cover art needs to speak to you personally.

The right cover should make an impact on you before it makes an impact on your target audience.

Set aside the preferences of your audience for just a second. Think about all those hours you spent on writing your book. Think about the ideas, the work, and the efforts you've put into it. Think about how you poured your heart and soul into this project. Does it feel personal now? This is how the ideal book cover should feel. It's your job to choose that special cover, which will fit your own written artwork perfectly. The key to a successful liaison between the cover and the contents of your book lies hidden in the fact that the cover should feel just as personal to you as the content of your story does.

3: THINKING YOUR AUDIENCE WON'T JUDGE THE COVER TOO HARD AS LONG AS THE

BOOK'S CONTENTS ARE WORTH IT

How will your audience know if the contents of your book are worth spending time and money on if they don't even pick it up?

Imagine this: you're walking into a bookstore and you're heading towards the shelves with your favorite literary genre. Are you going to pick up every single book on those shelves just so you can read through every single summary on the back covers? Of course not! You're going to pick up the books with the eye-catching covers.

Believing in the good old saying that you shouldn't judge a book by its cover is a mistake every author is prone to making. The right cover is the one that depicts the exact atmosphere of the book. Your potential readers are most definitely going to judge your cover and they are going to build expectations about the book based on the visuals. They are going to skim through the résumé only after the actual cover has made an impact on them—such a strong impact that it has made them reach out towards your book. Don't make the mistake of believing your back-cover blurb will sum up your book—the cover of the book needs to do the same.

4: NEGLECTING YOUR AUDIENCE

Your audience has a pre-established idea of what the covers of a specific genre look like. Not taking your audience into consideration and neglecting that built-up image is a huge mistake.

You do want your cover to be appealing and to look like it really belongs in your genre—not as if somebody has taken it from the other end of the bookstore and has randomly misplaced it on the wrong shelf, thus mixing it up with the wrong genre. Think about your audience and your target group. What are they looking for in a physical or in an online bookstore? What are their preferences? What are their expectations of the covers in their favorite genre?

The best-selling book cover for your project will be the one which meets those expectations and at the same time stands out from the standard generalization. You want your cover to be distinguishable from the rest, but you don't want it to look like it belongs to another genre, otherwise you're significantly lowering your chances of getting people to buy your book.

5: CHOOSING THE WRONG COVER ARTIST

Hiring a professional cover artist and spending a fortune doesn't automatically guarantee a best-selling product.

Spending countless hours in communication, tons of cover art drafts and misunderstood explanations will engage both you and your designer into a whirlwind of headache and annoyance, a great amount of time blown to waste, and worst-case scenario—a final result, which is just not good enough. Your job is to write the best-selling contents of the book and the cover artist's job is to come up with the best-selling digital art. However, the problem when hiring a cover artist for a unique custom design is that regardless of said cover artist's skills and qualification, that person will never be able to fully depict the idea you have had for your book and your cover on a one hundred percent match. No cover artist can see through your eyes, mind, and vision, or illustrate your own idea of your perfect cover as accurately as your imagination is doing it.

A winning bet when choosing your cover artist is to opt for a pre-made book cover.

Why are pre-made covers better than custom-commissioned covers? Browsing through a catalog with pre-mades gives you a brilliant example of how your choice of a cover will look next to other covers from the same literary genre. Will it be too plain? Will it look out of place? Will it fall into the right category just perfectly? Pre-mades will answer all of these and many other questions in an instant. Here are some additional advantages a pre-made book cover offers next to a custom commission:

- It spares you from wasting your and your designer's time with tons of drafts, long hours of communication and a possible clash of interests.
- It's significantly faster.
- It gives you the best insight when comparing various covers.
- It has a fixed price.

A custom cover might cost you anything between $100 and $2,000. Every discarded draft will cost you more, every new alteration will annoy both you and your cover designer, every additional hour of miscommunication will set a potential playground for conflict and headaches.

Choose the right cover artist and the right cover art wisely, because they will represent your book before your audience. The cover will speak for you and your story long before your book's resume and synopsis have had the chance to impress your readers and to transform them from potential buyers into actual fans.

---

*This article was used with the express permission of *thebookcoverdesigner.com*

DAVID WIND

CHAPTER FIVE
STEP 5
Formatting for eBook and for online sale

Formatting... *Arrrghhhh,* **the bane of a writer. Creative writing is one thing; the technicalities of formatting is quite another. eBook formatting is not difficult, but if this is your first attempt, you may want to use a professional.**

Didn't you already do a chapter on formatting?

Yes, but this chapter allows me a chance to show you how the pre-editing formatting becomes part of the final formatting for publishing. This method of formatting is both stylistic for the programming and stylistic for the book's layout as it deals with headers, footers, page numbering, lines per inch, and much more. Once properly done, your style sheet will be ready for your next book, including steps two and five, which means you've just saved a bunch of time and money.

However, if you really don't want to do this yourself, (many writers don't) and you have an editor, check to see if he or she will do this as part of their editing service. If not, formatters can be found easily with an online search, through a writer's organization, or by recommendation. Either way, having a properly formatted and edited book will help your sales.

In the beginning I used a formatter and was happy to let him do my final edited draft. Sadly, he passed on, and I decided to do the work myself. After having used him for five novels, I had a much better understanding of the formatting for eBooks and print books and was able to set my style sheet properly for eBook formatting, so when I wrote, I was writing within the proper format and would only have to make a few adjustments.

There is a particular way for your book to be formatted, not just from the technical aspect, but from the visual. Most Indie authors want their books to look like the books published by traditional publishers. The natural way to do so, is by following their example, but only to the degree you believe necessary.

DAVID WIND

The differences between an eBook
and a traditionally published book
can be found in several ways.

The Table of Contents, for an eBook is usually the last page(s) of the eBook, because it is not directly referenced while reading; rather, the eBook reader is programmed with a link to the Table of Contents, so it is reachable from any page. Another notable difference is the author's ability to add hyperlinks to the book, linking to other pages within the book, or to pages on the Internet, or even e-mail addresses. (The Trad publishers have begun to follow our footsteps.)

One further difference that distinguishes most Indie eBooks from their traditionally published authors is in having the TOC at the back of an eBook novel, it allows more pages for the 'Read Inside' feature on the major retail websites. An extra two to three pages of the story helps. Of course, you can and should put the Table of Contents at the front of your print version. For non-fiction, the Table of Contents should go in the front of an eBook and print book.

For eBooks you do not need the same formatting as you would for print books: *page size* is unnecessary, as are extraneous *page margins.* Skip *hyphenation,* as the eBooks wrap around. Many people do not bother with *page numbers;* I do. Many don't use *headers*; again, I always do. I believe the header should be set up the way you want. Either way works.

The end of one chapter and the beginning of the next should be done with a *PAGE BREAK,* even if the page ends on the last line. When the eBook is converted into the proper programming, the page lengths will change.

Let me add a quick note. When I format my manuscript at the start of my project, I plan to use the same final edited manuscript for both print and eBook. The formatting is similar, with certain changes from eBook to print. But the 'basic' formatting setup should be used until that point.

When you have finished the entire process and are ready to unload your manuscript to the publishing site or the aggregator, make a copy of the manuscript and add the word PRINT to either the front or the back of the file name. Then it is time to move the TOC to the front (if you are keeping a TOC) and you are ready for the final adjustments.

Suggested composition of your eBook by page type

PAGE 1: TITLE PAGE

Keep it simple: Title, Author, publisher—at bottom of page (if you've set up an LLC or a Corporation).

PAGE 2: Copyright and legal information

Copyright date, ISBN number (not essential in eBook) Cover Credits, Editing Credits.

PAGE 3: Acknowledgement (If there are acknowledgements)

PAGE 4: Dedication

PAGE 5: Secondary Title Page

This one is the simplest: Title and Author.

Prologue or Chapter One

All Chapters

Epilogue (if needed)

About the author

A short bio with a picture is nice.

Review Request

Ask the reader to review your book. Look at the back of this one for an idea.

Previous Books (if applicable). This is your bibliography.

Preview of the next novel (if applicable)

For books two and onward: The cover and one or two chapters, depending how long each is. This is an integral sales tool. There should be a BUY LINK at the end of the preview, even if it is only in Pre-Order. For pre-order previews, if you don't yet have a cover, then you will skip it.

Table of Contents (TOC)

The next thing you need to do, is to view your document with ALL the formatting marks visible. Why? Because you need to know how everything works together. To do this, you will use the 'paragraph' formatting icon in the tool bar.

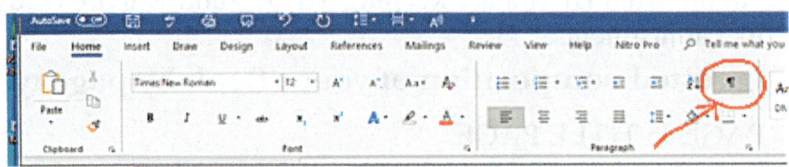

Once activated, this will show you all formatting marks, which allows you to visually maintain the integrity of your book's formatting.

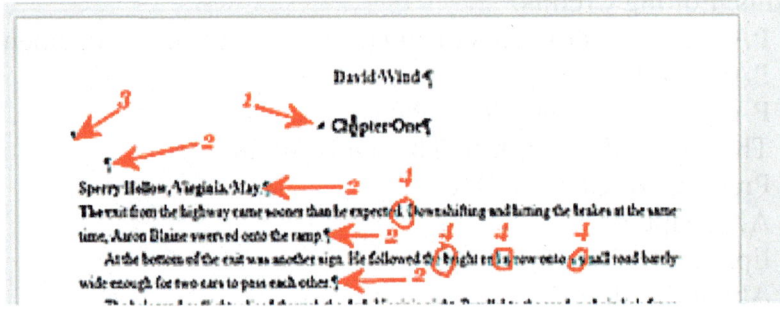

Notice how everything is not only visible, but it obstructs nothing. When you get used to working this way, you'll find out just how easy it is to do your work.

- The triangle (1) signifying a chapter header.
- Paragraph marks (2) are at the end of each paragraph.
- Formatting mark (3) signifying a header.
- Space mark (4) between words.

I will set down the basics for the final formatting into an eBook, but please, please remember, the simplest formatting makes for the best formatting. By keeping it simple, you offer your reader a smooth reading experience. Fancy formatting, with different-sized characters and fonts tends to draw your reader away from the story.

I am giving you the basics for MS Word, but remember, these are only the basics, some of which were shown in chapter two. You'll find a few links at the end of the chapter to websites that have more detail in a step-by-step how-to.

#1: Using MS Word, set your **NORMAL** style setting. The recommended style for eBook NORMAL, is either Times New Roman, or Arial. All the font settings can be accessed on the initial dialogue box.

- Font: Times New Roman, 12 pt,
- Indent: First line: 0.3", Left.
- Line spacing: 1.5 lines, Widow/Orphan control, Style: Show in the Styles gallery.

(I re-adjust the line spacing on my final draft to somewhere between 1.15 and 1.5, depending on the size of the book. Line Spacing is set in the next section).

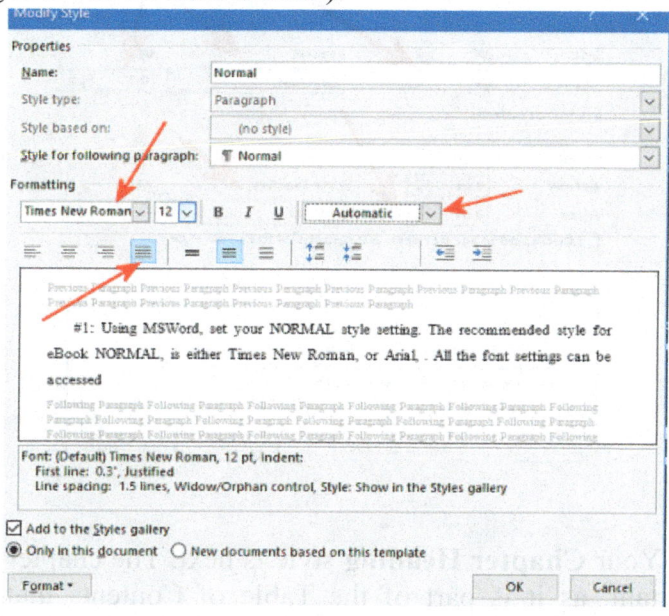

~#~

#2: Your **Paragraph** style setting is done to maintain a uniform paragraph throughout your work.

With the **NORMAL** style dialogue box still open, click the **FORMAT** drop down and select **PARAGRAPH.**

Then click the **SPECIAL** drop down in the Indentation section.

The first line of the paragraph indent will be perfectly uniform throughout your manuscript. Here is where you set the initial line spacing for the manuscript. You can change this later.

Click First Line in the Indentation drop down.

Set indent to either 0.3 or 0.5 using the *by* drop down box, either select or enter the length of indent: 0.3 or 0.5.

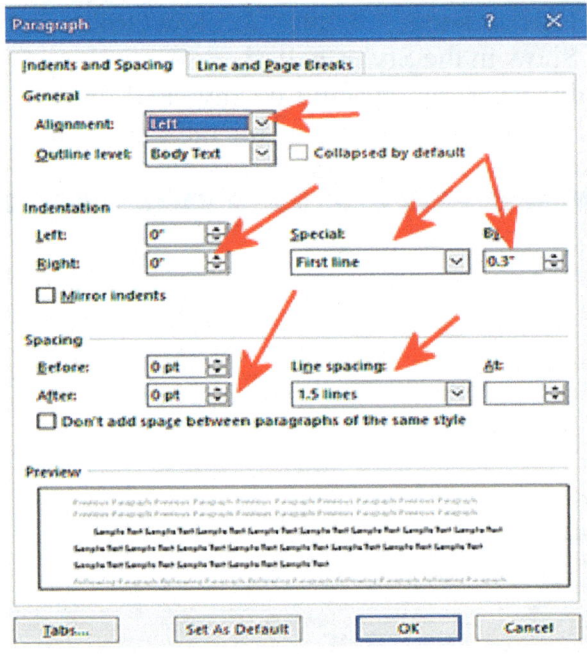

#3: Your **Chapter Heading** style is next. The chapter heading is important, as it is part of the Table of Contents that will be created both, by MS Word and by the conversion to the ePub and/or Mobi files.

The header style is your choice; however, do try to stick to the traditional fonts already in Word, for two reasons: Because utilizing the Chapter Header (or Header 1) makes your later added Table of Contents work better; and, use the traditional fonts of Word in case the eReader your reader uses does not have the new or fancy font imbedded in its programming. If you need to use 'special' fonts, then they must be imbedded into a PDF, rather than uploading a Word doc.

I use:

- Garamond, 14 pt, Bold, Text 1, Indent:
- First line: 0", Centered, Space
- After: 6 pt,
- Style: Linked, automatically update

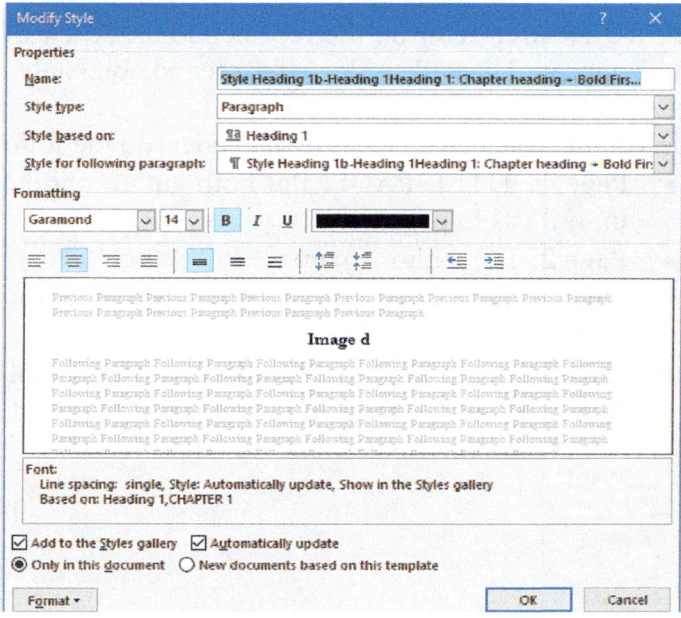

If your book is non-fiction, you should set up HEADERS 2,3,4, etc. to be the sizes you want on paragraph headers.

~#~

Your page headers and footers should be done as follows: As you can tell by this book, I use the title on one page, my name on the other, and the page number on the bottom of the page.

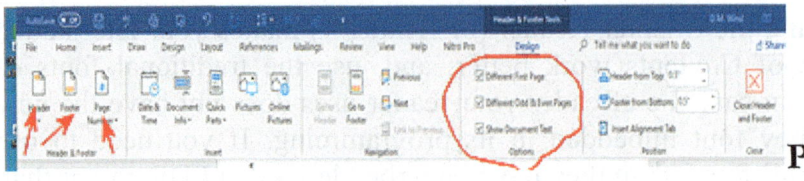

PAG

E HEADER—How To

Right click the top of the page to open the header menu, then,

- Check off — Different First Page
- Check off — Different Odd & Even Page
- Check off — Show Document Text

Set your header on the pages themselves, starting with:

Click the **Header Icon** on the top menu bar. A list of header setups will appear. I usually select the second, but only use the center.

Once you have selected the style of header, do the following:

- Page 1: TITLE PAGE. Put both author and book title in, if it fits to page.
- Page 2: The author's name .
- Page 3: The book title (Try to keep everything on a single line.)
- Then click on the Page Number icon in the tool bar and select where you want the number to go. I always select the center bottom of the page.

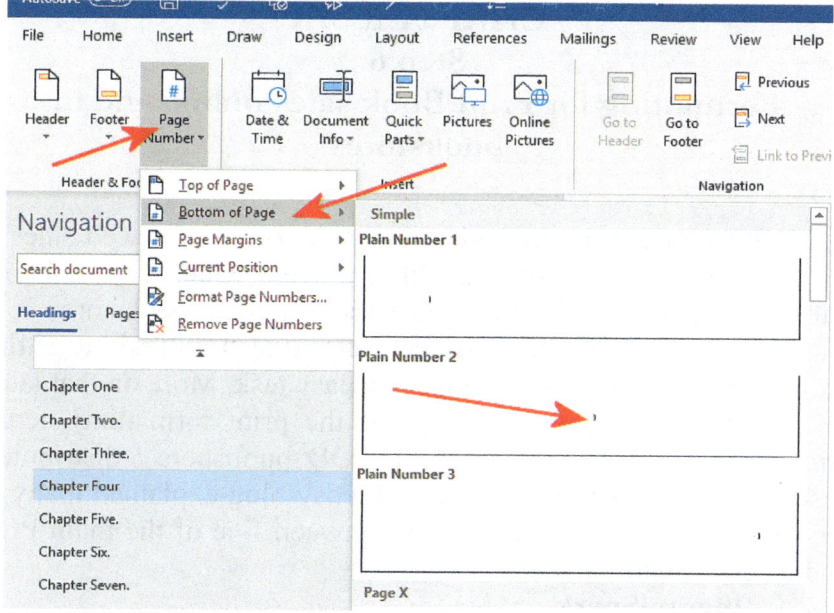

These are the basic settings for formatting an eBook in Word. From this point on, things should be fairly simple. A quick page-by-page scan, looking at the formatting and how the headers and chapters fall is your last step in the formatting. Once you are happy with the results, and you've built your front page and back page matter, you are ready to go.

CHAPTER SIX
Step 6
Formatting for Print Book sales online and in bookstores

Having your eBooks and print books online for web sales is the first part of the print publishing process. Getting your books into bookstores, both Indie bookstores and chain bookstores is as important, and should be considered essential. I will admit getting Indie books into chain stores is not an easy task. More on that later.

Before we get into the meat of the print formatting step, I think it's important to discuss the POD publishers / distributers first. There are several of them. A Reedsy blog explained many of the similarities and the differences between five of the main POD publishers/distributors.

IngramSpark
KDP Print
BookBaby
Blurb
D2D Print (Beta)

To get a full explanation of each, I recommend you read the Reedsy Blog I referenced, which is titled, *What is the Best Service for   Print   On   Demand   books?* (https://blog.reedsy.com/print-on-demand-books/)

I use IngramSpark for all my POD, except for books sold on Amazon, where I use KDP Print. I've found IngramSpark, for my purposes, to be the best print distribution for bookstores and all bookselling websites, except Amazon.

My reason for using two separate POD sources is based on distribution, costs, and royalties. While Amazon's KDP print is excellent, (and fairly easy to set up and publish) and while their internet reach is extensive, far too many bookstores do not like dealing with the company they believe is hurting their overall business. Be that as it may, this is not an argument for us at this time; rather, the reality for a writer is in the royalties. Amazon's

Print On Demand sales, and therefore the royalties on those print books, are extremely poor outside the Amazon websites and Amazon brick and mortar Amazon stores. IngramSpark's reach into bookstores is deep, and their royalties are better from bookstore sales.

Ingram also gives the Indie writer/publisher the opportunity to offer bigger discounts to the bookstores as an incentive to carry the Indie writer's books. An Indie writer can also specify that like a traditional publisher, returns of unsold book can be permitted.

Ultimately, as a professional writer, it is incumbent on you, and you alone, to decide which companies to use for your Print On Demand books.

With all of that said, the work saver here is that you already have a perfectly (we hope) formatted eBook, which means you are only a few steps away from a perfectly formatted Print-On-Demand manuscript.

As with eBooks there are always more than just a single POD format; however, I believe that like eBooks, the basic formatting of the manuscript is the same. This means we can create a formatted manuscript for Amazon and IngramSpark out of the same manuscript. (With some minor changes as to links in the manuscripts' before and after pages.)

You can also download the templates from each of the publishers and build your range of publishing knowledge further. I've found most Indie writers prefer to use the 6 x 9 format. This size is usually referred to in publishing terms, as a *Trade Paperback*. Trade refers to the 6" x 9" finished size of the book, which is also a similar size to many hardcover books.

While I publish all my paperbacks in Trade size, I know several writers who prefer to do the more traditional paperback size. Whichever size format you use, the only differences in the page setup, are in selecting the page size itself as part of the formatting.

For this step, we'll open the formatted manuscript. When the manuscript is fully loaded, CLICK SAVE AS, and save THIS FILE as (whatever your title is + the word PRINT). Now you have your eBook manuscript saved and can work on the first of two print versions of the manuscript.

Go directly to the Word tool bar: click LAYOUT

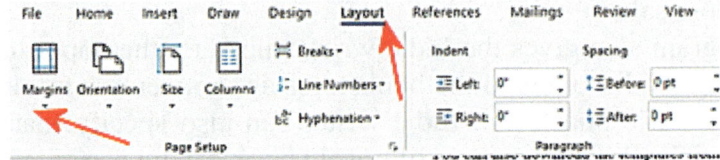

Click MARGINS. then Click CUSTOM MARGINS.

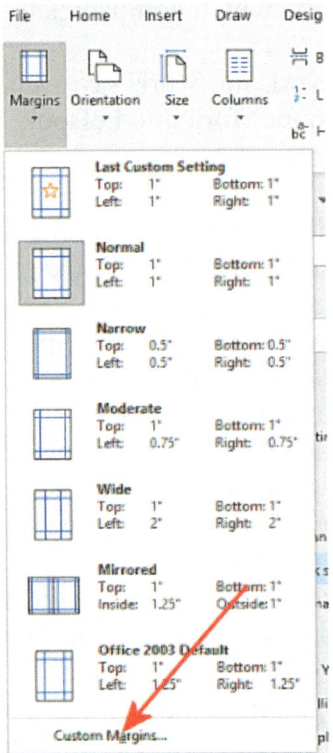

Once the custom margins link is clicked,

a new dialogue box opens.

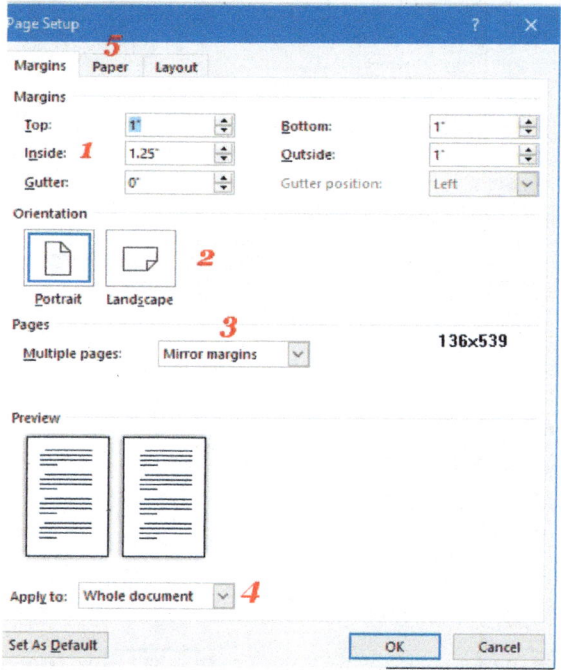

This dialogue box is where you set your margins, which for a print book are set up for opposing pages. After setting the margins (1), in the Orientation box, select PORTRAIT if it is a regular book page (2), then select MIRRORED MARGINS in the pages box (3), so that the margins match properly for inside and outside pages. Then set PREVIEW to Whole Document (4), if it does not already show selected (should be default).

Next, click the Paper tab (5)

to open the new dialogue.

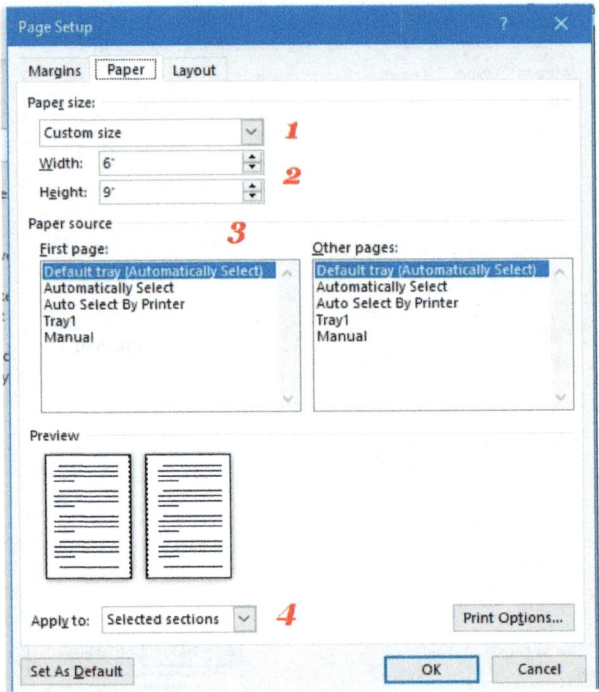

Once opened, select (1) CUSTOM SIZE, then set your PAGE SIZE (2), then set the PAGE SOURCE as shown (3) and make certain the APPLY TO is set for selected   sections (4).

Next, click the Layout tab to
open the new dialogue.

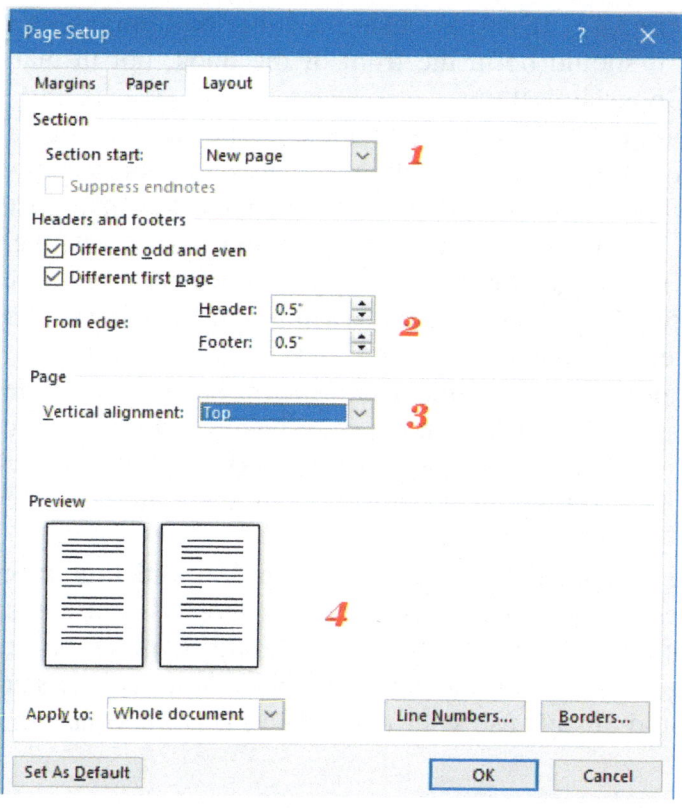

Once opened, select NEW PAGE (1), then make certain to check the boxes for DIFFERENT ODD AND EVEN, DIFFERENT FIRST PAGE, and the HEADERS set from 0.35 - 0.5 from edge is selected (2), then select VERTICAL ALIGNMENT as TOP (3), and finish with (4) Apply to WHOLE DOCUMENT. Then click OK, and your manuscript is set.

With your manuscript's basic formatting now set, you have a few more decisions to make. Which POD publishers should I use? (For purposes of this book, we will use Amazon's KDP Print and IngramSpark). What changes will I need for the front and back matter?

Change #1: If you are using a Table of Contents in the print version, it should be in the front of the book, not in that back as many eBooks are set up.

Change #2: You need to look at the number of pages and determine if the way the book is formatted is good, page-wise. If it is a big book, you should check to see what the final cost to print will be. If the cost is too high, leaving you a relatively small royalty, my suggestion is to make your line space less—between 1 and 1.15/1.25 to make the book affordable to a larger readership, and to keep the bookstores interested.

Change #3: Front and Back Matter changes would be to have URLs (spelled out fully) in the paperback for a reader to use to go to your website, profile pages on BookBub, Amazon, and others. Once you've settled these items, you are ready to … as they say … rock!

The formatted manuscript for Amazon and IngramSpark can be shared (with some adjustments) as long as you are not using either of their ISBNs, as the ISBN should be noted on one of the title pages along with the copyright info. And, as I've said earlier, you should always use your own ISBN, it is important in the long run.

FRONT MATTER
- PAGE 1: TITLE PAGE- Keep it simple, Title, Author, tag line. Set publisher name at bottom of page (if you've set up an LLC or a Corporation).
- PAGE 2: Copyright Page; legal information, copyright date, ISBN number, cover credits, and editing credits.
- PAGE 3: Acknowledgement Page (if there are acknowledgements).
- PAGE 4: Dedication Page (if any).
- PAGE 5: Secondary title page. This one is the simplest: Title and author. (Having this is a sign of a professionally published book.)
- TOC: Table of Contents: Use only if you believe it is necessary. Chapters with numbers only don't give the

reader information. Chapters with titles usually work best.

BACK MATTER

- About the author Page: a short bio with a picture is nice.
- Review Request Page: Print or eBook, ask the reader to review your book. Look at the back of this one for an idea.
- Previous Books Page (if applicable).
- Preview of the next novel: this is an excellent marketing option, but it can add to the costs by the addition of the preview pages.

Once the print manuscript is ready, it should be converted into a PDF, which is then uploaded. Converting to a PDF also gives you one more chance to make sure all aspects of the manuscript are right. If you find an issue, it's an easier fix now than later.

Converting the manuscript into a PDF is not really difficult, and if you have the correct software, the work will go smoothly along. I use Nitro Pro. I've found it easy and it integrates with Word, so everything can be done from the same Word document I'm working on.

What I've shown you in the preceding pages is my method of setting up a print manuscript. There are other methods. But, remember, I recommend for your first book at least, to use a professional formatter who will format for both eBook and Print. Usually the price for doing both is either the same as for one, or just slightly higher.

Both KDP Print and IngramSpark have templates for you to download. Once downloaded, you can 'pour' your manuscript into the template by copying your manuscript in its entirety and then pasting it into the template. The pages will flow. You fix any issues, and then convert the templated manuscript into a PDF and you are off to the races.

With all of that said, there is a 'shortcut'. Draft2Digital offers a PDF download of your manuscript that is technically ready for Amazon or IngramSpark; however, I have found that doing it myself seems to work with fewer hitches and reformats.

THE MOST IMPORTANT THING TO REMEMBER ABOUT PRINT BOOKS, is that your cover for each POD publisher/distributor is a different dimension. However, your cover artists will make the right size for each, using the POD's required template—it's what they do!

And again, if you decide to go against advice, doing a print cover for Amazon and IngramSpark will require a large amount of work and graphic knowledge.

Here are three reasons why I use both
Amazon and IngramSpark for Print.

- Unlike Amazon and Barnes and Noble, that sell directly to customers, IngramSpark does not sell directly to the public. They are a distributer and (like eBook aggregators) will place your PRINT book into most online bookstores as well as brick and mortar stores.
- Amazon will sell your book on their sites (and in their stores if your book sells well online); however, in the extended sales to bookstores, they only give a 40% discount to the bookstore, a much smaller royalty to you, and do not offer returns
- Unlike Amazon, bookstores order your book directly from IngramSpark, booksellers require strong wholesale discounts, the ability to return books, and most bookstores prefer not to buy from their largest and most antagonistic (according to them) competitor— Amazon.

CHAPTER SEVEN
STEP 7
The ISBN
(International Standard Book Number)

Let's start with the basics: ISBN is the acronym for **International Standard Book Number**. Until the end of December 2006, ISBNs were ten digits in size. Beginning January 1, 2007, they were increased to 13 digits. ISBNs are calculated with a specific mathematical formula and include a digit, known as a check digit, to validate the number. An ISBN identifies a specific book, an edition of a specific book, and/or a book-like product (example: audiobook).

The purpose of an ISBN is to identify one title or edition of a title from a specific publisher, with a unique identifier to that edition, allowing for more efficient marketing of products by booksellers, libraries, universities, wholesalers, and distributors. In an everyday explanation an ISBN is many things to almost every person and business within the publishing industry from creating to publishing to selling and yes, to buying books.

As the Internet sales grow, and as more and more ancillary businesses are finding ways to sell, use, or promote books, those businesses and people will be requiring the use of an ISBN to keep track of their inventory and sales.

Now that you've got that down pat, here's a curve ball: You do not have to buy your own ISBN. You can use the ones offered by Amazon, iBooks, Barnes & Noble, Draft2Digital, Smashwords, etc. However,—and this is important—from the moment you take their ISBN, you are part of their publishing/distribution 'label', and not your own. (This is a simple explanation. You can look up more detailed information online.)

I have and use my own ISBNs, which I purchased from Bowker, the licensed vendor for ISBNs.

For Hybrid authors, having your own ISBN on your backlist books to which you have your rights returned to you is an important step, because you now have the ability to make a decision that can and most likely will affect the future of your work.

Will you re-publish the book exactly as it was, or will you update it? This question is one not lightly asked, as you will need to make it a second edition (or third or whatever) with a new ISBN, and if the changes are that significant, you should add a new copyright.

I've updated several of my earlier Thriller and Mystery novels, which were written before cell phones reached their prominence, forensics was old, and many of the laws outdated; but there were no plot changes. While these second editions had changes, none were significant enough to require new copyrights.

So, Hybrid authors, the choice will be yours, as an Independent writer/author/publisher. Enjoy it!

ISBNs for eBooks

So, the next logical step in the publishing process, is the acquisition of ISBNs for your book. This then asks the question; will this be my first book or my only book?

If it will be your only book, be it fiction or nonfiction, you need only purchase a single ISBN number for your *eBook*. If you plan on writing three or more, it is much more economical to purchase ISBNs in blocks of ten. The difference is significant. ISBNs, at the time of this writing, are $125.00 each; however, if you buy a block of ten, the cost is $295.00, which brings the cost to $29.50 per ISBN—approximately twenty-five percent of the cost of a single individually purchased ISBN.

This is a no brainer for anyone planning to build a writing career, or at the least, put out three books, or two books to be published in both eBook editions and print book editions. Each type of book, eBook, or Print must have its own ISBN.

As I stated earlier, this is not a step-by-step how-to book on publishing, it's a guide to help you become a professional Indie

Writer/Author. For ISBNs, however, I think it's important for you to understand the process, so we will do a little step-by-step here.

How do I get my ISBN for an eBook?

Go to Bowker Identifier Services https://www.myidentifiers.com/Get-your-isbn-now, sign in and register an account, and then go to the main page, where you select the ISBN package you want to purchase (one, ten, or more).

Once the purchase is complete, you click the MY ACCOUNT button on the toolbar, then select MY IDENTIFIERS from the drop-down menu.

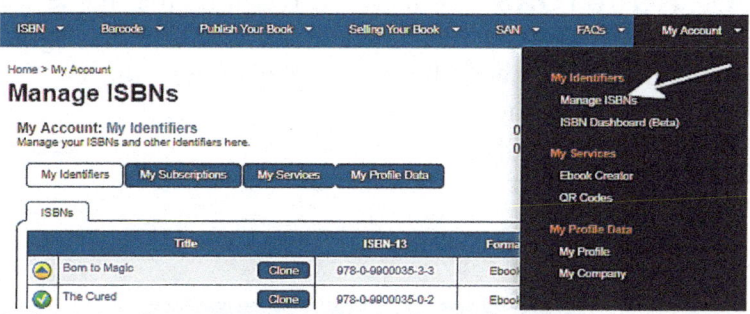

Select the first ISBN number, click it, and you are taken to the first of four input screens, **Title & Cover.**

Each form page has sections that must be filled out. None of the pages need be one hundred percent filled out; rather, the ones with the red stars are the only required fields. Having full information in the Bowker database is also a positive, so I suggest you put in as much information as possible.

TITLE & COVER only requires the title. (I do Title, Description, Cover, and date of publication, language, and intended copyright.)

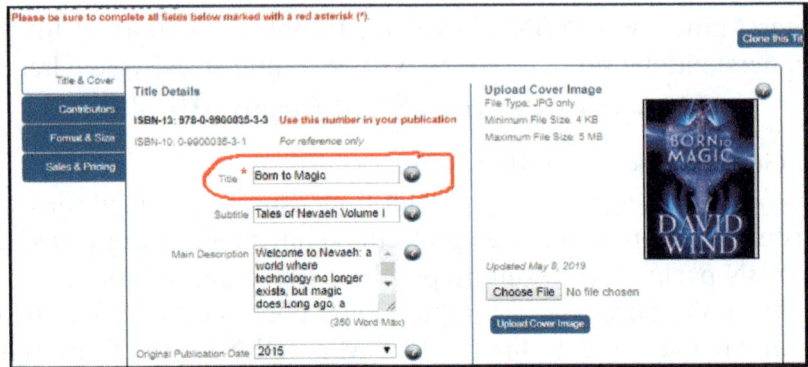

(Image shows only top half of page)

CONTRIBUTORS Form Page requires the name of the author, if that is you. If not, select your role on the right-hand column. You can also add the writer if it is not you, or if it is a collaboration or an anthology.

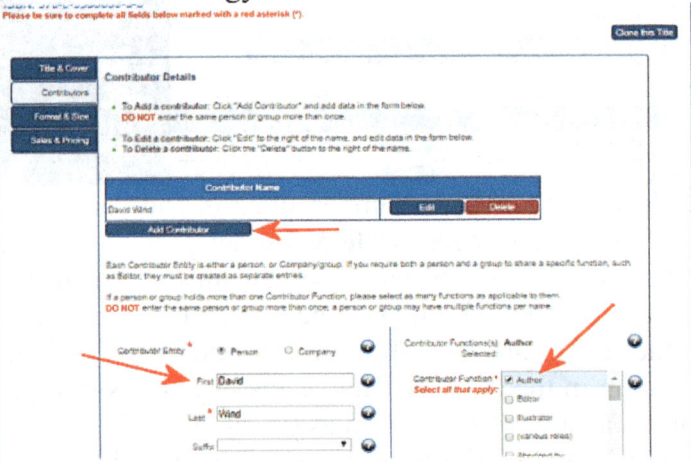

(Image shows only top half of page)

FORMAT & SIZE only require the medium (eBook) and the Format (Electronic Book Text). This form is the main difference between eBook and Print books.

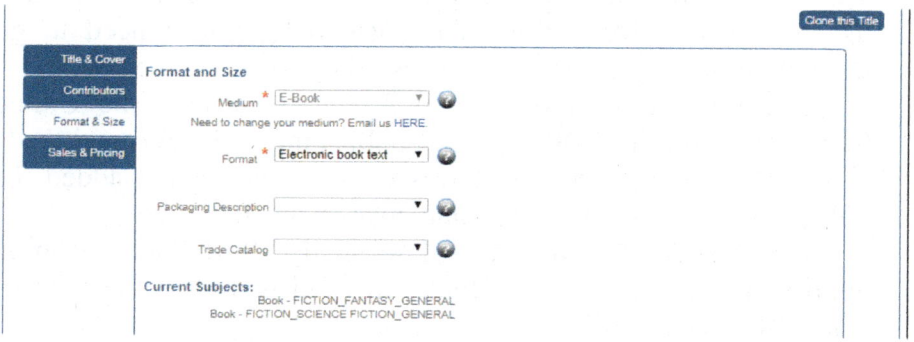

If you have decided to put out a SECOND EDITION with significant changes for a book you already have an ISBN for, then you will need to fill out another section on the **FORMAT & SIZE.**

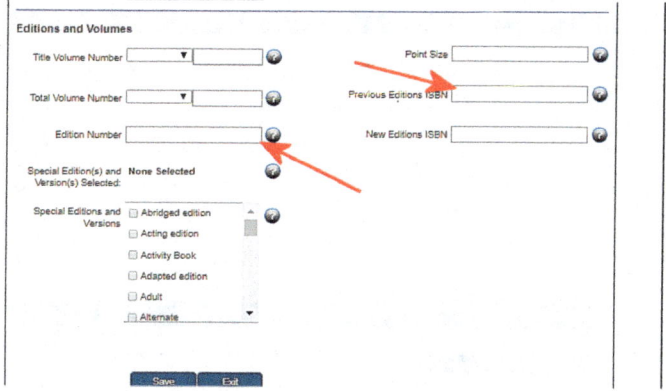

Once this is done, it's time to move on to the final screen.

SALES & PRICING form page has seven (7) required areas to be filled in. These are the minimum. The next image shows my Sales & Pricing form for which I only filled in the minimum, because I am registering for U.S. sales. International sales can be done through the aggregator or retailer or distributor. If you are going to sell your books directly to the public, then you'll need to do some additional work that we will not go into here.

On the form, fill in where you are selling. If it's the U.S., then use that. If it's for a foreign country only, you'll need to go through those fields, which are accessed by selecting the country.

Using my form for *Born to Magic*, I selected the United States, then used my DBA for my publishing of DMW, and made it an active record because it was coming out soon. I added the publication date and my target audience to finish part one.

Part two deals with money. I selected U.S. dollars, put in an approximate price for the eBook, and finished with the type of price I showed, Retail.

The **Submission Button** is next and, if you did it right, you were greeted with a success dialogue box and you are done!

Once you've finished here, copy down both your ten-digit and thirteen-digit ISBN numbers, and keep them available to use.

You'll need them. And then you're off to the PRINT ISBN, if you are going to have a print version of your book.

ISBNs for Print Books

POD—Print On Demand books have many POD publishers available. Most of them offer you the availability of their ISBN. Again, easy to do, no work, but whose book is it then? Yours of course, but they own your ISBN. As I've said before, buy your ISBN. And, if you publish or plan to publish as I do, with multiple POD Retailers/distributors, your own ISBN means you can use it with any aggregator or distributor you select. If you use their ISBN, you'll be given a separate one for each company you deal with.

There are two differences between the eBook version and Print version ISBNs. The first difference is found on the **Format & Size** page. The first difference is the Medium, which will be **PRINT**, then comes the Format, which is **PAPERBACK**. Then you have the option to fill in size. Since my novel is a Trade Paperback, its size is six inches by nine inches. Then I move on to the last form page.

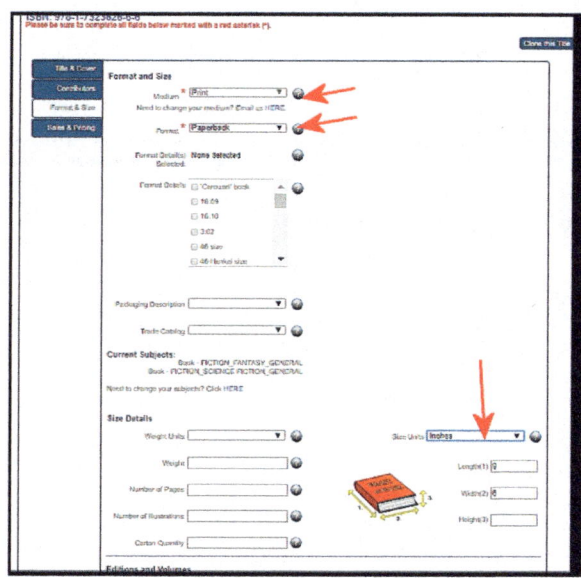

SALES & PRICING Form: The top section is the same as in the eBook; the middle section is where there is a change, and basically, it's only a price change. The sales information is the same in the top section, the change is exclusively in the middle area only on the price. What will your price be for the paperback?

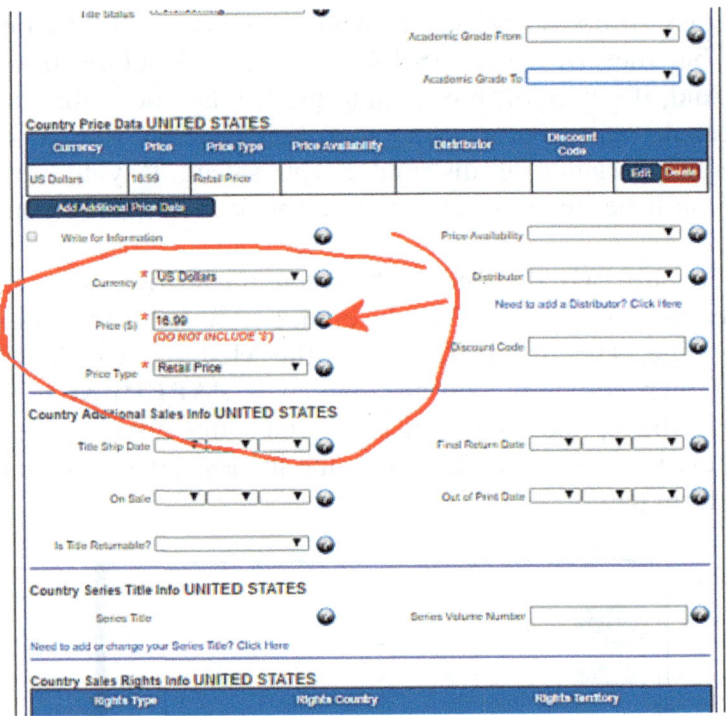

And now you are ready to move on.

CHAPTER 8
STEP 8
The Copyright

Copyright is a form of protection provided by the laws of the United States to the authors of "original works of authorship" that are fixed in a tangible form of expression. An original work of authorship is a work that is independently created by a human author and possesses at least some minimal degree of creativity. — The U.S. Copyright office (https://www.copyright.gov).

There are many reasons for copyrighting one's work: legal protection and proof of ownership forms the basis for copyrighting.

Being a professional writer, an Indie professional writer, means it is your responsibility to make certain all the details about your work are handled properly: one of those details is to protect your work.

"Are copyrights important?" you ask. Using a one-to-ten chart, they come in at about one hundred. Yes, copyrights are important. The main purpose behind the origination of the copyright law was and still is to promote progress in arts and sciences by protecting the right of authors to benefit from their work. In the case of publishing, it protects the author while allowing a wide offering of the author's work to the public.

A copyright protects your words, your sentences, your paragraphs, and your chapters, which are, in fact, your Intellectual Property. Registering a copyright with the United States government's copyright office helps to legally protect you from other people's plagiarism, unapproved use of dramatic rights, and in general, the theft of your work.

HOWEVER, there is another aspect of the copyright law you should know. You don't have to do anything to copyright a creative work. That's correct, your book is automatically copyrighted from the moment you put it into a tangible form, such as a finished manuscript either on paper or on a computer. But—

and this is important—if it is not a complete work, then it is not automatically copyrighted—and you should take another thought into consideration. The way laws work, and the way they change, can affect you at any time. It is better to be copyright-safe, than to risk the loss of your Intellectual Property, so:

WITH ALL OF THAT BEING SAID, COPYRIGHT YOUR WORKS FORMALLY AND LEGALLY! One of the issues of an author's copyright is to prove the date of the finished work. Many people send their manuscripts in a sealed envelope, certified mail, to themselves. They store it away, unopened, until it's needed.

I did the same thing until I realized the downside of not formally copyrighting my work. Without the protection an author's copyright offers, the burden of proof is upon me, and proving ownership of the work can cost me the legal expenses if I need to litigate the issue. When I publish with traditional publishing houses, they handle the copyright process for me. As a hybrid Indie writer and publisher, I do the copyrighting myself for all of my Indie works.

By legally registering a copyright, you are ahead of the game. So, the next step in the publication process is to register your copyrighted material with the government's copyright offices.

What a copyright does for an author is to treat creative work as a type of property—intellectual property. You can own a home, a car, a computer, and you can also own your creative endeavors like books, screenplays, poetry, and illustrations, by registering a copyright. The most significant difference between personal property ownership and intellectual property ownership is that *personal property* is yours for as long as you want to own it; while a copyright of *intellectual property* has a seventy-year life span.

To sum things up, you (and your work) receive a higher degree of legal protection when registered with the U.S. Copyright Office. The registration creates an official record of the work, the copyright owner, and the date of registration. The registration itself is an important legal consideration and sets grounds for any dispute coming about by the improper use of your copyrighted material.

On to the process

You can choose when to copyright your book, before it is published or after. As a professional in the publishing industry, and when possible, following the way traditional houses go through the publishing process is always recommended. I've never heard of a traditional publisher copyrighting an author's work after the book has been published, unless someone screwed up, and that could be something very dangerous to the publisher and the author.

Always choose to copyright prior to publication, it makes your job easier.

###

The Copyright Act defines "literary works" as "works, other than audiovisual works, expressed in words, numbers, or other verbal or numerical symbols or indicia, regardless of the nature of the material objects, such as books, periodicals, manuscripts, phonorecords, film, tapes, disks, or cards, in which they are embodied." 17 U.S.C. § 101 From the U.S. copyright office at https://www.copyright.gov/registration/literary-works/.

To start your registration go to the U.S. Copyright office's ECO (Electronic Copyright Office)— [https://eco.copyright.gov/eService_enu/start.swe?SWECmd=Start &SWEHo=eco.copyright.gov)] where you will need to register yourself first.

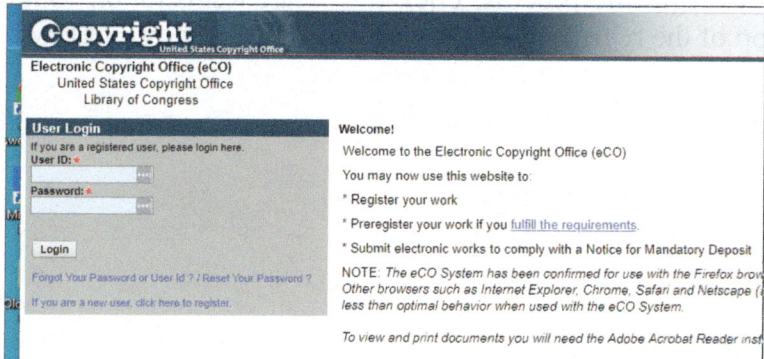

Once registered go to the home page. There, click to register a new work.

When you have clicked on Standard Application, the next page tells you what you will need, which is relatively simple. Your personal info, a credit card, and the ability to upload a manuscript.

To Complete the Application for Registration you must:

1) Provide all required information on the application form.

2) Pay the required fee.

3) Upload or mail in a copy of your work.

(To preview what you need, go to their FAQ page at https://www.copyright.gov/eco/help-registration-steps.html.)

To begin the process, click the 'Start Registration' button at the top of the registration Home Page, which is shown below.

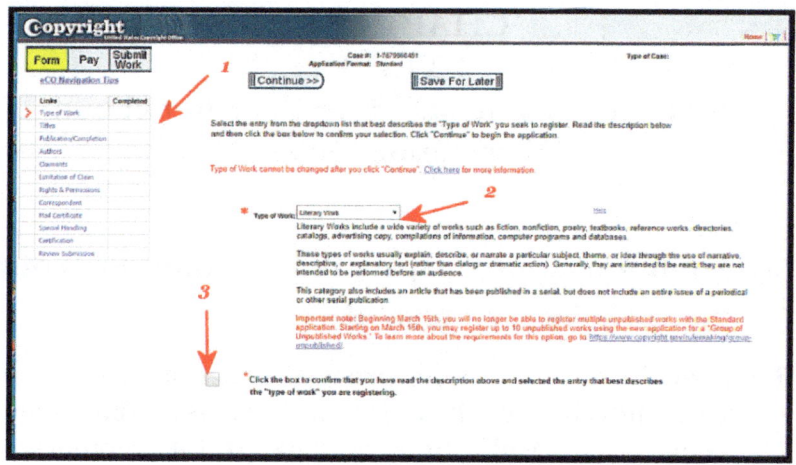

Step 1 is the type of work. I set the #1 arrow to show you there are twelve steps in this part of the process.

Step 2 is to select the type of copyright you are seeking. When you use the drop down, select Literary. The text explanation will automatically fill in.

Step 3 is to acknowledge you have read and understand the explanation.

Then click either CONTINUE or SAVE FOR LATER.

###

At this point, following the copyright process will get you safely through. It usually takes several months to get the hard copy of your copyright, but it will be protected once the copyright office follows through with your application, which is usually just a matter of a few days before you get the official notice.

In any event, *ALWAYS* place a copyright on your copyright page (see chapter 5) by using either: [copyright] [Year] by [Author Name]; or, [©] [Year] by [Author Name]; or, [© copyright] [Year] by [Author Name].

CHAPTER 9
STEP 9
Publishing: Understanding Your Retail and Distribution Outlets

Pay Attention: This Chapter Is Important for Your Wallet!

At this point in the publishing process, you should know who you will be publishing through initially. But that doesn't matter. This is the right time to look at the retailers and aggregators (eBook distributors) again.

Which retail outlet and which aggregator are always one of the toughest questions within the Indie publishing process and, if you are anything like me, this will continue to haunt you and you will make ongoing changes. Tweaking may be a better word—think about changes as tweaking within your publishing process to enable you to build a wider audience for your books.

Let's begin with a breakdown of the differences between retailers, aggregators, and POD distributers as well as the leading retailers for the eBook and Print Book (POD) industries.

eBook Retail / Online Book Retailers

An online publishing company selling the books it has published through its own retail store is categorized as an *eBook retailer*. Examples include Amazon's Kindle Direct Publishing (KDP) and KDP Print (POD), Apple's iBookstore, Barnes & Noble's Press (POD) and Nook, and Kobo are the "big names". Many of these companies have built partnerships to distribute books to other retailers for the print books they publish and sell, such as KDP Print's Expanded Distribution program.

Aggregator: eBook Distribution

An aggregator is an online eBooks distributer. Several of these aggregators offer more than just the distribution of eBooks to their partner online retailers and libraries; they have their own retailing platform as well. (Smashwords, Lulu), and their own promotional arms and author services. This helps Indie writers to step outside the boundaries and restraints of Amazon or iBooks and put their eBooks into wide distribution. There is another aspect of aggregators, which allows for the distribution of eBooks to outlets authors cannot submit directly to. Scribd is one example of a reader subscription service not accepting eBooks directly from authors.

Aggregators can be used without ever having to submit directly to Amazon, Apple or Barnes & Noble. That is your choice. I prefer to submit to Amazon and Kobo directly, and use the aggregator for submissions everywhere else, including Apple's iBooks. I don't work on an Apple device, and until recently, one of the requirements for submitting directly to Apple was to use an Apple product to do so. Recently, Apple made changes so a PC user can submit through the iCloud.

I submit to Amazon directly because it allows me to take advantage of their promotional offers. I submit directly to Kobo, because they have a deep reach into many European, Asian, and African countries. But, again, be aware that once you go 'wide' you can lose some of Amazon's promotional advantages.

Print On Demand Distributors

Although we use the term *aggregator* in place of *distributor* the term only applies to eBooks. We use the term *distributor* for companies producing print books (POD) for brick-and-mortar stores, online retailers, libraries, and schools and colleges. The print distributors, such as IngramSpark, and "hybrid" *aggregators*, like Amazon, Lulu, and BookBaby both distribute and offer retail sales for print books, while distributors like IngramSpark do not retail books themselves. However, the overlap within companies like Lulu and BookBaby, that retail both their published eBooks and POD books and wholesale to brick and mortar outlets, means they can technically be called *distributors*. Yet, IngramSpark remains a pure *distributor* because they do not sell retail; they only distribute books—even those they publish as eBooks.

OVERALL

In our industry, the Independent writing and publishing industry, the number one spot goes to the 900-pound gorilla. Amazon is, from all the statistics I've seen and heard, the largest retail bookseller in the world. That said, Amazon's KDP is the number one online eBook and print book retailer.

This doesn't mean your book can't do well on other retailer sites; rather, it means you must make a choice. Do you publish exclusively with Amazon or do you go 'wide', as we Indie writers say? Going wide means you must make a decision to give up certain benefits which Amazon provides to the 'exclusive' authors. These benefits vary, depending on how well your book is selling on the Amazon websites.

Going wide versus using Amazon exclusively

There are several advantages for using Amazon exclusively. It is the world's largest book-selling platform, they will pay you seventy percent royalty (less download fee of a few pennies) for every book priced at $2.99 or above, and you can use Kindle Unlimited, where the Amazon members pay a flat monthly fee and read as many books as they want. On KU, you get paid for every page a reader reads.

Be warned, if you go wide, you will lose Kindle Unlimited. Some writers live exclusively on their KU earnings, but you need to build a hell of a readership audience for that. As an example, say you have 10,000 pages read one month. Sounds like a lot, doesn't it? Well, 10K pages pays somewhere between $40.00 and $44.00. The absolute best-selling authors also get extra bonuses, but here you're talking seven figures in pages.

How do the page reads compare to actual book sales? Say you have an average 75,000 to 80,000-word novel, about 325 pages. Using basic math, we divide 325 into 10,000 and come up with 30.75 books. If the book sells for the average eBook price of $2.99, which gives you a royalty of approximately $2.00, then your royalties from 30.75 books would be $61.00 (round figure). You do the math—10K pages $44.00 / 30 novels $60.00.

Going wide *does no*t mean you will automatically make up the difference from your page read losses by leaving KU; what it does mean is you are more in control of your works. In order to have control, you need to know who in the industry is who and what works best for you. And the only way to find out what works best, is the tried and true method of experimenting with all avenues open to you.

The Top Ten Retailers and Aggregators

eBooks

#1: Amazon KDP*** (Kindle Direct Publishing) — Online Retailer

The number one spot goes to the 900-pound publishing gorilla. Amazon is the largest eBook seller in the world. That said, Amazon's KDP is the number one online eBook and print book retailer.

Amazon is usually the first retailer where most Indie writers decide to sell their works. According to *The Balance Small Business* a 2019 article shows Amazon sold seventy-four percent of the eBooks bought in the U.S. in 2015.

Amazon also has KDP Select, which is an exclusive part of KDP. To be on KDP Select, and to be able to benefit from Kindle Unlimited, you must agree to be EXCLUSIVE on Amazon to be part of and profit from the Kindle Select Program.

Cost to publish:
- Price: Free to upload
- Royalties: 70% if the eBook price is between $2.99 and $9.99, under $2.99 it drops to 35%.
- Print or eBook: Both. (It is important to note Amazon reduces royalties for any eBook over $9.99 from 70% to 35%.)
- eReader: Kindle and Kindle derivatives and apps for other devices

~#~

#2: iBooks — Online Retailer

iBooks by Apple is the next largest retailer after Amazon. To publish directly on iBooks, you must either have an Apple device, or if you use a PC, you must go through the Apple cloud; however, you can easily publish through an aggregator, which is what I do.

Cost to publish:
- Price: Free to upload
- Royalties: 70% Flat rate
- eReader: iPad, iPhone, computer. (ePub format)

~#~

#3: Barnes & Noble Press

Barnes & Noble used to be called Nook Press. Almost all Nook eBook sales are in the U.S.

There is not a lot to say about B & N.

Cost to publish:
- Price: Free to upload
- Royalties: 40-65% based on the price of the book
- eReader: Nook, iPad (ePub format)

~#~

#4 Kobo[***] — Online Retailer

Kobo, an anagram of the word book, is the fourth largest eBook retailer. Kobo is a true World-Wide retailer of eBooks with Kobo-published eBooks available in over 190 countries. Kobo is also a powerful player in Canada, with close to a quarter of the eBook market. Kobo also maintains partnerships with eBook retailers world-wide.

Cost to publish:
- **Price:** Free to upload
- **Royalties**: 45% or 70% based on the price of the book
- **eReader**: Kobo has their own versions of eReaders as well as apps for cell phones and tablets. (ePub format.)

~#~

Aggregators and eBook Retail Aggregators

#5 Draft2Digital (D2D) — Pure Aggregator

In the spirit of disclosure, Draft2Digital is my aggregator for all eBook retailers except Amazon and Kobo. It is also the aggregator I recommend. They will format your book into an ePub, or a Mobi, and you can even download a finished PDF.

As a pure aggregator, D2D does not retail eBooks; and, while D2D has fewer retail partners than does Smashwords, it does distribute to Amazon and all major retailers.

Draft2Digital also offers several author benefits: Their Universal Book Links (UBL) is a major benefit. Draft2Digital's *Books2Read.com* produces a single web page link (Universal Book Link) for each of your books. This link allows a potential reader to select whichever retail outlet they use for their book buying and takes the customer directly to their preferred retail website.

D2D also offers its *automated back matter* tool. By checking off whatever items you want included at the back of your book, like *Author Biography, New Releases,* and *Books by this author,* it will automatically add the pages to the back matter of your newly published eBook.

I have spoken with the folks at D2D and they have assured me there will be a print option coming in the near future, but they did not venture a date.

- **Price:** Free to upload
- **Royalties**: D2D charges 10% of the retail price at most retailers. So, for most retailers you will average royalties of around 60%

Note: Draft2Digital offers a support page loaded with referrals to Editing, Cover Design, Marketing, Author Advocates, and Directory Services—they do not offer the services themselves.

~#~

#6: Smashwords[***] — Aggregator, Online Retailer

To my knowledge, Smashwords was the first full aggregator and continues to be popular. It distributes eBooks to most all retailers, including Kobo, iBooks, and Barnes & Noble, but not

Amazon. Smashwords and Draft2Digital offer similar pricing structures and royalties. And while Smashwords has a slightly larger distribution network, the formatting aspect of Smashwords can, to many of us, be difficult. You must have your book fully formatted to their specs, which are close but not quite the same as Amazon or a few others, and their support on formatting is light.

When I started to go wide for my book sales, I used Smashwords, and still maintain an account. It is a good aggregator with many benefits. Their creator, Mark Coker, is not just a trailblazer in the aggregator world, but one of the most knowledgeable Indie supporters I have met. He writes an informative newsletter and keeps us all up to date on what is happening in the Indie writing industry.

Additionally, Smashwords also retails your book(s) on their website; has promotional abilities and offers special discount coupons you create and offer out. These coupons (coupon codes) can work wonders when doing giveaways and promotions without using any of the major retailers. The coupons can also be used to give reviewers and beta readers their books.

- **Price:** Free to upload
- **Royalties**: Smashwords takes 10% of the retail price of your book on the Smashwords retail channel, and 15% of the retail price at their partner retailers—this is in addition to the retailer's own fees

~#~

**For a well-drawn out comparison between
Draft2Digital and Smashwords
by Dave Chesson of Kindlepreneur, <u>Click Here</u>**

~#~

Print On Demand Distributors

#7: IngramSpark *** — Pure Distributer
This Print On Demand distributer was established by Ingram, the world's largest book wholesaler and the leading distributor of

print books. It distributes to 39,000 bookstores, libraries, and online retailers in over 150 countries.

They also publish hardcover books, and they offer a premium level of printing which is best for picture books. Most importantly, IngramSpark offers you the ability to have a book returns option; Indie authors who use this option tend to have a better chance at competing for shelf space in the brick-and-mortar bookstores.

Ingram's costs vary, so you'll need to go through their website to know exactly what options you want to use, and they have some advertising and promotional services.

As I indicated earlier, IngramSpark is my primary POD. Distributor and printer.

- **Price:** Varies from $50-$98 (But do look for coupons, they are usually available.)
- **Royalties:** Depends on your discount to bookstores. (A 304-page book, 6" X 9" in size, with a 50% bookstore discount will return a base royalty of approximately $3.00.)

*Two important notes about IngramSpark: (1) If you want your print book distributed to all major non-Amazon online retail websites, they are the best option; and (2), I see their eBook distribution as more of a necessary convenience for their authors than a dedicated aggregation service but that's just me

~#~

#8: KDP Print — Print on Demand / Expanded Distribution

Amazon's new platform for print books using Print-On-Demand publishing is KDP Print. They have closed down the original POD program, CreateSpace. KDP Print retails exclusively on Amazon, unless you join the Amazon Expanded Distribution program. With the expanded distribution, KDP Print lets Indie authors make their books available to other online retailers as well as brick and mortar bookstores and through distributors such as Baker & Taylor and Ingram, IngramSpark's parent company.

- **Price:** No charge

- **Royalties:** 40% royalty for Amazon retail sales. Expanded distribution varies, see note

Note: For some, the issue with Amazon's expanded distribution, which after deducting Amazon's 60% commission, a fixed charge, and a per-page charge from the book's list price makes for a very small royalty

~#~

Print On Demand All in One

~#~

#9: BookBaby*** — All in one eBook Aggregator/Print Distributor/Retailer

BookBaby is an eBook aggregator, a POD distributor, and a retail sales site. BookBaby retails books in their 'Bookshop' and offers distribution to other retailers. Like all the aggregators, retailers, and distributers, BookBaby also offers extra services.

eBooks earn 100% royalties after deducting the retailer's commission. Sales made through Bookshop, however, earn 85% royalties. BookBaby also has a Print-On-Demand service. Printed books generate royalties between 10% and 30%

- **Price:** $299.00
- **Royalties:** eBooks earn 100% royalties after deducting the retailer's average commission of 55%-70%; Direct sales through BookBaby Bookshop earn 85% royalties

~#~

 # 10: Lulu*** — All in one eBook Aggregator/Print Distributor/Retailer

Lulu, one of the older online aggregator/publishers and popular distributor of digital and print books, retails your books in their bookstore, and distributes to other online retailers. They also distribute your print book to Ingram and Barnes & Noble. Lulu offers hardcover and paperback formats on print books. Lulu charges a 20% commission after deducting any book production costs applicable to print copies. Sales generated through partner retailers would additionally attract their own commission.

- **Price:** No charge.
- **Royalties:** 20% commission on the Lulu site: like Amazon, they charge a high distribution fee which greatly reduces your royalty share

~#~

Other vetted sites include:
Blurb
PublishDrive
Scribd
StreetLib
XinXii

~#~

By no means is what you have just read the only online retail outlets, aggregators, or POD Distributors. I suggest … no, I implore you to do your research, to learn about every available option, and then move forward. A second avenue, which you should not leave unexplored, is with the various list serves, from LinkedIn, to KDP Boards, to reading Indies Unlimited for columns articles and blogs on the Indie Industry. Using the ALLi blogs will also be valuable in deciding and consider joining a few online author groups—just make sure everyone on the group isn't a newbie like yourself.

Oh, please do your research before going on to Step 10.

***These retailers, aggregators, and distributors offer extra services to their authors, such as editing, cover and interior design, and marketing services. All of these services have fees.

THE INDIE WRITER'S HANDBOOK

CHAPTER 10
Step 10
Set up Publishing and Selling outlets

This next step should not be considered a how-to; rather, it is a discussion.

Let's assume you've gotten your manuscript back from the editor, and you've made the necessary changes. You've also gotten your ISBN for the eBook, and the ISBN for the print book if you are doing one. At this point, you should have either registered the copyright, or you're waiting for your paperwork to go through. Now it's time to move on to selecting and setting up your publishing outlets.

In the previous chapter, we went over a list of retailers and aggregators. Those are not the only ones. As I wrote at the end of the last chapter, my list of online retailers, aggregators, and POD distributors in no way contains all the retailers and aggregators. My list of outlets are the outlets I am personally familiar with from my research and use, or from the recommendations of other professional Indie writers. If there is a retailer or an aggregator you want to work with that is not on my list, I suggest you check the outlet carefully. Do your research, because once you put your book out there, you are no longer the only one who has some control over what happens.

This is the point where, as we move forward, you must decide on which outlets you'll use. Once you've made the decision on which Retailer(s) Aggregator, and Print Distributer(s) you will use, the accounts must be set up.

Without setting up your accounts, you cannot get to the beta readers or the reviewers, or even know which types of marketing to do until you have your sales outlets set and ready to publish.

DECISION NUMBER ONE

DAVID WIND

What should I use, Amazon exclusive or wide distribution? No one can answer that question except you. A lot of writers I know started on Amazon exclusively. There are excellent reasons for this, and excellent reasons to not go exclusive. What I've found to be eighty-five percent consistent when discussing this with either Indie authors I know or discussing it at writer organizations, is they use Amazon exclusively for the first three months and up to a year.

There is a plethora of reasons for starting on Amazon only: some start this way because they want to test the waters and see the sales response to their work; others because they believe Amazon is the largest market in the world and therefore the only one they need to concentrate on; and, yet others who want to see if staying exclusive to Amazon gains them Kindle Unlimited readership to make up for not going wide. These are all valid reasons, and should be part of your research, especially when talking to others in the industry.

What I don't agree on, is that Amazon can do it all. Understand, I am not anti-Amazon, in fact I am extremely pro-Amazon, and why wouldn't I be? Amazon is my biggest sales channel; however, adding the grouping of retailers from an aggregator will add more sales. Not everyone owns a Kindle, and not everyone downloads a Kindle app. There are an awful lot (multi-millions) of Apple users out there, reading on their readers, phones, and iPads. Then there's Kobo, which make even more of the English-reading countries of the world reachable to you. In fact, Kobo reaches a hundred and ninety countries.

When you publish your book on Amazon, especially those first three months, you will need to monitor how well the Kindle Select/KU feature works. (You will also need to do promos to let readers know your book is available.) One way to look at it is like this is if you have 100,000 page reads, you make roughly $450.00 in Kindle Unlimited page reads. This is the equivalent of approximately 300 book sales of a $2.99 book. Not bad, and different from the figures in the earlier chapters. The difference stems, of course, from volume.

If it drops lower and stays there, it is my opinion that it's time to consider adding other sales channels. But, again, you are the one who must make the decision. There is one bright side. If you decide to stop going wide, KDP select will take you back ... as long as there is not a single copy of the book available for sale anywhere in the world, other than Amazon.

Traditional publishing has always been a time-sensitive industry. Every month thousands—between six and ten thousand traditionally published books are published and distributed in the United States. This means the bookshelves must have space for the new books. Where do the old ones go?

The benefit we Indie writers have OVER traditionally published writers, is that we don't ever worry about shelf life. That's right, we don't have to watch our books show up in a bookstore, and then a month or two later, see all but, if you're lucky, one or two copies survive.

When you publish Indie, your bookshelf always has your books on it. Yes, I know traditional authors now have a similar advantage with the publisher keeping their book online; however, the publisher rarely does any marketing after the initial blitz (if your book rated high enough for them to even consider doing real marketing when it was originally published). So, the Trad writer then has to play catch-up and try to get their own marketing going, while the Indie writer has been marketing the book since (hopefully) long before publication—almost from conception.

Oh, and the traditional publishers have changed their contract with the advent of eBooks, so they have found yet another way to hold onto the rights of their authors' books even when the print versions sell nothing, which leads to the next paragraph...

...And the other great Indie advantage is that it doesn't make a bit of difference when your book was published. The book can be two, three, even ten years out of the gate, and your marketing can bring it to new readers every day, every week, every month, and every year!

Okay, I've digressed as I usually do, but not too far, so let's get back on track. You don't have to start out exclusively on

Amazon. There are many Indie writers who start with the big four from the get-go. It just takes more work, unless you use an aggregator.

If you have an Apple device, then I'd suggest you do Amazon and Apple individually. You can do Kobo and B & N, but to make it easy, if you do Apple and Amazon yourself, then you can use the aggregator for everything else.

If you do not have an Apple device, then it's just as simple. Set up Amazon yourself, then go through the aggregator for the others.

None of the retail sites are hard to set up, they just require the time to do it properly. On Amazon, register as an author with KDP. If you are going to publish on Apple yourself, follow the regular process for iBooks, and then move on to your aggregator.

What I'm trying to impress upon you by holding you here before going any further, is to make you see how pivotal a time this is in the publishing process and the very point where *you must determine* how you are going to publish your book—for at least the first three months. As I've already explained, research is the key. Research doesn't just mean sticking your head in a book and reading or going online and finding information. Yes, those two ways of researching will help greatly, but human research is important as well.

Talk to other Indie writers, look at their online posts, and respond appropriately. Look for a consensus of publishing methods and then decide which one you want to follow. I don't recommend experimentation for your first book. But, no matter what, you must decide now in order to move on.

What you need to properly register.

The list is pretty simple for Amazon:

- Your Country
- Your Name
- Your Address (FULL)

- Your Telephone
- Your Bank Account—the one you use for your book business
- Your Tax information (They call it the Tax Interview)

That is basically it. Personally, I use one name for my book business, and another for general purchasing on Amazon. Of course, it's your choice.

The other retailers are similar. They all must have your personal, bank, and tax information to proceed.

You can set up your main publisher(s) and your aggregator now, and you don't have to publish anything yet. When to publish is your call: the timeliness is on the aggregator. Draft2Digital and Smashwords both have more intense setups than do the retailers, because they are, in turn, setting up more with their retail partners.

Both require full personal and business info, then each goes into what they do for you as far as perks, and the information you enter sets you up completely on their internal and external systems, which in turn will set you up for their sales partners, so take your time and do it right as it will make life easier as you progress.

Your aggregator is also the perfect place for you to get downloads of your eBooks in different formats. Both Smashwords and Draft2Digital will allow downloads of Mobi, ePub, and PDF files, so you will have books for your beta readers and reviewers in whichever format they require.

There are a lot of marketing uses for your ARC books, so don't think your need of these ARCs is over with beta readers… Your marketing needs will require them as well.

Having completed the setup for publishing, it's time to get your first final draft uploaded. Okay… What's a first final draft…?

CHAPTER 11:
STEPS 11a & b
Pre-Publishing Upload and Beta Readers

>Pre-Publishing Upload/11a

>Beta readers/11b

Finding beta readers should be considered a requirement for Indie publishing. Beta readers are much more than someone who gives you their unprofessional opinion, which is exactly what you want. A beta reader is a reader who is not a specialist in publishing, but a specialist in rendering an opinion on what they like to read! Let's just say the perfect beta reader *is a professional reader*.

In order to get the book into a beta reader's hands, you want to have a finished copy of the book, in a Mobi or ePub format. The last thing you want to do is send an electronic manuscript to your beta readers to read on their computer! Therefore, you must do what I call a half-step, so consider what comes next step 11a, and after that 11b.

The Pre-Publishing Upload (Step 11 a)

What is this?

The pre-publishing upload is a simple step that should not take more than twenty minutes, if you've done everything right until now. So, let's check on that. You have formatted your book for editing, then had your cover commissioned, and formatted for eBook and Print. Then you purchased your ISBNs and went through the copyright application process.

In Chapter 9, you learned which retail outlets, aggregator, and distributor you can avail yourself of. For an example, let's say you start off with one retail outlet, and one aggregator. We don't need print, yet.

As I've mentioned before, while you may already have accounts, and even books published, I am treating this guide as one for first-time writers as well as experienced and published Indie and Traditional writers..

I will use Amazon (our 900-pound gorilla) as the retail outlet, and Draft2Digital as the aggregator. If you have not yet set these outlets up, do so now by registering as an author on Amazon KDP, and as author on Draft2Digital.

Once you have your account(s) set up, it's time to pre-publish your book. You start the process on your BOOKSHELF page, by clicking the Create a New Title Kindle eBook button on your bookshelf page.

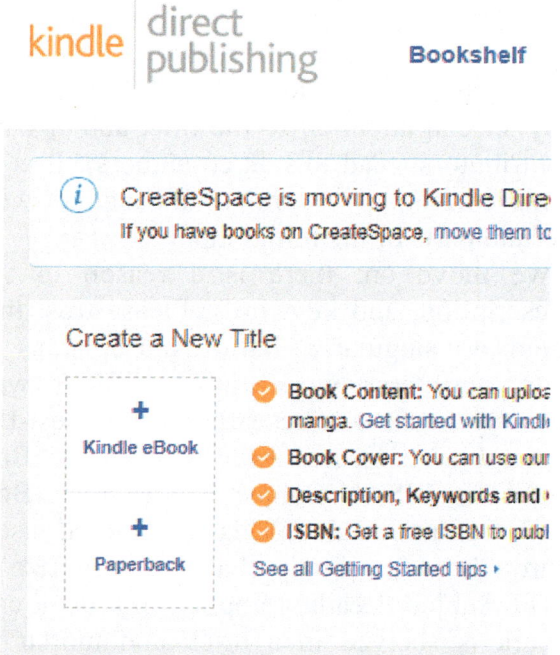

Once clicked, the browser will open on the Kindle eBook Details page. You will now fill out *mos*t of the information.

At this stage, leave the **description, categories, keywords/key phrases, and ages** of readers blank. You'll get to those later after you've done your research for these sections. The goal in this step is to complete the eBook creation process and have a viable **ARC** copy of your book to download.

An **ARC** is an Advance Review Copy or Advance Reading Copy. It is a complimentary copy of a new book given to reviewers, booksellers, librarians, journalists, celebrities, beta readers, and/or others before the book is published and available to the public.

When you fill out the information, DOUBLE CHECK EVERYTHING which means to copy edit your responses to the questions. Pay special attention to the title, author name, and any additional contributors (read this as co-authors). It is important to get these items correct, as several of the outlets will not allow changes to certain parts of the initial input.

Before we move on, there is a reason to wait for the categories, description, and keywords. Please trust me on this as these three items are singularly vital to your book, as is everything you've put into your literary work, but in a different way.

The reason you wait is to research out the best BISAC codes to use for your book's genre. According to the Book Industry Study Group, 'The BISAC Subject Codes List (Book Industry Standards and Communications), is a standard used by many companies throughout the supply chain to categorize books based on content. The Subject Heading applied to a book can determine where the work is shelved in a brick and mortar store or the genre(s) under which it can be searched for in an internal database.'

Amazon, on the other hand, does not use BISAC codes. Amazon uses their own categories, many of which match BISAC codes, but others do not specifically match BISAC codes. This means the BISAC code you use, Or in KDP's case, the AMAZON CATEGORY you use will determine where the book is shown, both in bookstores and on the Internet's bookselling websites.

Another item to note about BISAC codes is that BISAC codes are also used by search engines to return specific books in those categories, which also means you can use BISAC codes for SEO on your websites.

The other important metadata needed to be entered on that screen will be the description and keywords and key phrases to enable the retailer's searches to find your book. Hence, the need for research to determine which category and keywords are best. We cover this subject in-depth, in the following chapter.

From this page, you move on to the Kindle eBook Content page, where you now enter everything.

Starting with (**1**) the DRM question. DRM is Digital Rights Management. This is a method of preventing your book from being copied and resold or given to others. This is a decision you need to make. But research it out, as any professional will do.

Next, (**2**) is why we are here! Upload your manuscript. Once you do, their ePub conversion software will go to work. When it's done, (**3**) it will tell you if it found any issues, among them is misspellings. We'll get to the proofing aspect in a moment.

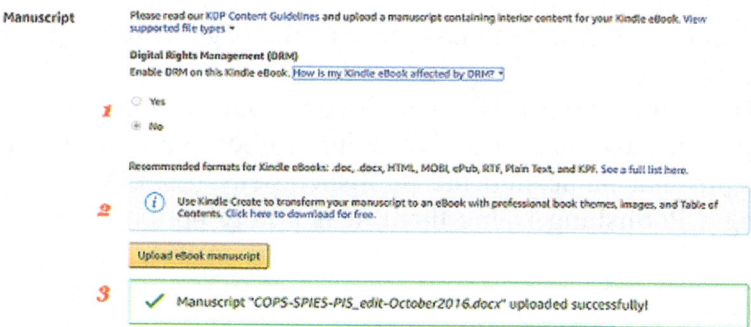

Before proofing your "galley" the next step will be your cover. As I've explained, if you are a professional Indie writer you will have a cover from your cover artist. If you decide to do it yourself, KDP does offer a cover creator, which will create generic covers, but again, unless you are also a graphic cover artist, be smart, be a pro, and use a pro!

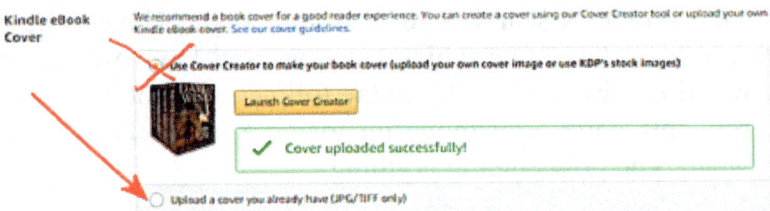

Further down on the page, you will find the area where you can proof your book online, or download a Mobi copy or a HTML copy. I find the Mobi to be the easiest and use my Kindle program on my desktop to proof. This is the point where you would fix the errors. HOWEVER, if the program does show errors, I use the online proof program to locate them so I can quickly correct the errors, rather than use a Kindle or Kindle program to find the errors.

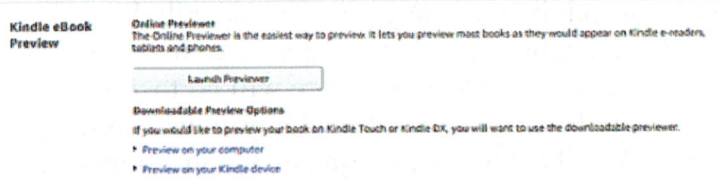

Finally, we reach the last piece of the page, entering the ISBN and publisher.

If you have your ISBN, which you should, put it in now (**1**).

If you have started a publishing corporation, partnership, or LLP, put that name into the publisher field. (**2**) While I prefer having a Publishing Name there, it is purely optional for an Indie writer.

Kindle eBook ISBN	ISBN (Optional)
	Kindle eBooks are not required to have an ISBN. What is an ISBN? •

1 | ENTER YOUR 13 DIGIT ISBN NUMBER HERE |

Publisher (Optional)

2 | *My Publishing Company* |

Unless you are going to do Pre-orders (which should wait until the ARC copies have been read), click the SAVE AS A DRAFT button. I urge you to consider that pre-orders rarely work out well unless you've got a proven track record of sales and the readers who are anxious for your next book and willing to buy it now and wait up to ninety days for the release.

If you've done everything needed for this section, then we are set for the pre-publishing, and the production of your ARC Mobi file and it is time to talk BETA READERS!

STEP 11b
Beta Readers

First off, the answer to your unasked question: Yes, we writers have stolen the use of "BETA" from the software people of the world, so consider a beta reader the literary version of a software beta tester.

To get a better feel for a real definition of what a beta reader does, I offer you the Wikipedia definition of beta reader:

'A beta reader is usually an unpaid test reader of an unreleased work of literature or other writing, who gives feedback from the point of view of an average reader to the author. The beta reader is not a professional and can therefore provide advice and comments in the opinions of an average reader. The writer uses this feedback to fix remaining issues with plot, pacing, and consistency. The beta reader also serves as a sounding board to see if the book has had the intended emotional impact.'— Wikipedia

While Wikipedia does a great job of telling us what a beta reader is, I have a few caveats to put forth. First off, and this is important, a beta reader does not mean just anyone. *It means someone who is NOT your friend, and who is NOT a family member.*

As hard as it is to accept, you should not have anyone who will not be truthful give you their opinion (positive or negative), unless they are a professional in the publishing industry, and then they are NOT a beta reader.

You ask why, and I can honestly tell you it's because <u>most friends will lie to you</u>! This doesn't mean they're being cruel, or your work isn't good; rather, the lies come usually for one or more of the following reasons: the most common reason is they like you and don't want to hurt your feelings; or they do not read books in your book's genre, and do not know what is good or what isn't good in the genre.

As I've said, there are a lot of reasons, but one overriding factor is friends will read your book, whether it is in their genre likes or not. If the friend finds it 'readable' they might say, 'It's better than most of the junk out there', which you may take to mean it is good. But, do you want a book that's better than most of the 'junk' out there, or do you want to hear, "I liked it, it's really good."?

Of course, we all want the second, but if the book is out of the reader's genre wheelhouse, what do those words really mean? *Is the friend being honest?* Does your friend know publishing and if your book, in its particular genre, works as well as do the better books of that genre? The real answer to these questions is, the person is your friend, take the words with a smile and a grain of salt, and know you have a friend who wants to help. What needs to be done is relatively simple. Find someone who reads your type of book and ask them to read yours. Tell them you are asking because you want honesty, plain and simple. This isn't easy because most don't want to cause hurt, and honesty can do this, which is why I, and many of the writers I know and work with, feel the same. It is the reason we work with beta readers who we do not personally know, but who are avaricious readers, and who like being in the forefront of a writer and their newest books.

It also saves them a ton of money, because they read what we call **ARC** copies of books. **A**dvanced **R**eading **C**opies. These readers, will, if you ask them, also post reviews when the book comes out. (We'll discuss reviews later.)

But how do you get a beta reader? That's a loaded question. There are many ways, and there are many services as well.

My friend and fellow Indie writer, Amy Vansant, created Authors Cross Promotion [https://authorsxp.com/]— an Indie writer marketing service. Within the AXP program, Amy has a beta reader-finding service to match genre-specific beta readers with writers of their genre.

Goodreads has a beta reader group, which the group's tagline is, "A place to connect writers with beta readers." Click here to check it out.

Facebook has several groups, Beta Readers & Critiques, Beta Readers, and Beta Readers and Critique Partners. There are more, but these should get you started. Just remember to ask the right questions about genre … it's always about genre when you seek a beta reader.

Please do take into consideration that I am not recommending the above services and groups to you (with the exception of AuthorsXP, which I do use); rather, I use them as examples of how to find beta readers.

A beta reader does much more than read. They critique your work. The beta reader goes through the book, thinking about all the books of your genre the beta reader has read, and makes their decision based on the experience of a book reader, and their own gut reaction to the story. The beta reader also looks at specific aspects like *suspension of disbelief,* for novels, or the *viability of the presentation* of the information in a non-fiction book.

The beta reader *critiques* the pace of your story, the *interest level* through all the pages, the way the *characters act and react*, and the *pace of dialogue* as well. A good beta reader will also keep track of typos, misused words, and my beta readers have, at times, queried why I used a specific word they didn't know and had to look up—do keep in mind that knowing the readers within your genre will help to guide you in how you use your grammar and vocabulary.

I have a memory from a writers' conference, that was burned into my mind. There were a group of us signing books at the end of the third day. The author next to me (a well-known author who will remain nameless) smiled happily as a short, broad, and stubby woman stepped to her table. The woman half placed; half slammed a book down in front of the author. She planted knuckle-fisted hands on the table and leaned her barrel chest forward like a bulldog.

"You have a lot of nerve. You don't use a high fa-lu-ten word to describe how to pick up a bucket and a mop, why did you use them to describe a romantic scene. You ruined it for me!" She straightened up, turned, and walked away, leaving the book behind.

I took that lesson to heart. If the writer had simply used two or three beta readers, the embarrassing scene might ever have occurred.

Once your beta readers have given you their opinions, and you're secure in your work and what you've learned from the readers, then, if you really want to, you can give a couple of family or/friend readers the book to "beta read". Again, only if you really want to, and only if you're sure you can accept what they say, and then apply the old cliché ... *a grain of salt.*

THE INDIE WRITER'S HANDBOOK

CHAPTER 12
Step 12
Early marketing Strategies

As a professional Indie writer, author, and publisher, early marketing is not only essential, it is crucial: the strategies you employ, and the timing of every step in the process is significant and important.

Exactly what is early marketing strategy?

Early marketing is getting word out ahead of the book, just as traditional publishing houses do for their biggest-selling writers. Although you don't have the *New York Times*, or *Publisher's Weekly*, or any of the massive national book publications to work with; you have something just as powerful—social media outlets. Yes, you have Twitter, Facebook, Pinterest, Instagram, writers' and readers' literary blogs, and a host of others.

Social media is a good part of your advertising and marketing arm, and a dominant one. HOWEVER, you need to take into consideration how much marketing is done online and in social media. To prepare for this, you should open specific author accounts. As a professional writer, using your personal accounts is not always in your best interest. You will also find some of your personal life will spill over into your author life, but to start, keep business and personal as separate as possible.

Why do I say keep your author's account separate from your personal accounts? Let's look at your Twitter account and use it as an example for social media accounts in general. If you use your personal account, do you want friends and family to see what readers have to say day after day? It won't always be pleasant. And do you want your readers and fans to get deep looks into your friends and family? Then you say, "But I have a thousand followers on my personal account, isn't that a good base?"

Of course, it is, but you don't have to lose that base, just ask them to follow your new account, explaining that one is personal, and the other is to spread the word about your books. If they sign up, it gives you the opportunity to thank them for helping to spread the word and make your books popular with their retweets on Twitter and for posting and sharing on Facebook, etc. Not too many friends or relatives would deny you this little bit of help, especially of it doesn't cost them anything other than a few keystrokes.

Let's go through the process: create a new account on Twitter, such as JonSmithauthor. The first thing you'll need to do is to follow others. Many of those will follow you. Start tweeting about the area of interest of your book, and as you pick up followers, you'll find those who share your interests (or your book's interests at least). Unless you have written a book on politics, I'd suggest skipping any political comments or commentating. Readers are funny in how they perceive other people's political ideology. Do what you want on your personal Twitter page but keep your book page sociable.

After a few weeks of tweeting about interesting subjects that will lead to talk of your book, it's time to make the first mention of a book you have coming out soon. Give the title, and a few (very few) words about it—don't overdo it!

Do not think you need to do this all day long. Two, maybe three times a day is enough. Too many tweets, posts, etc., and people will not be happy. Keep it slow, low, and easy. You don't want to be labeled a spammer.

If you start several months ahead of the book's release, I recommend a ninety-day advance period for early marketing, and by the thirty days before release, you start pushing just a bit harder on all social media fronts.

At this point, it's time to think about some advertising. If you have the budget for advertising, where you spend it should be based on how you are releasing your book. Is it starting out as an Amazon exclusive? If the answer is yes, then at the sixty-day point, you should have joined at least ten to fifteen Facebook Book Kindle oriented groups (this is a minimum suggested amount) and have gotten into occasional conversations with the members, again always focusing the posts toward your book's subject. The same should be done if you have joined Goodreads.

If you are starting out wide, then join more Facebook general book groups, and those specifically dealing with the genre of your books, but not necessarily Amazon-leaning groups. When I say genre-leaning groups, I mean book groups that focus on Thrillers, Mysteries, Science Fiction, Fantasy, or if you write non-fiction, books that deal with your book's subject.

At the thirty-day pre-launch point, it's time to start posting once a day, about your forthcoming novel. A short description—almost an elevator pitch—to get them thinking about the book. Also, make a bit of a big deal about the "cover reveal" at the thirty-day point, and start showing your cover. Remember, no more than once a day on these groups, and not more than three to five groups a day in the beginning.

I am a member of several dozen Facebook groups, and post twice a day, to different groups with each posting. I have enough groups so as not to repeat posting on the groups more than once every seven to ten days. And if I post more frequently, I use different titles.

When you have several books available, you can set up a posting schedule for yourself. It is more work, but over time, it sells more books. I will run a single title through all my groups over a ten-day period, say starting on a Monday. Then on a Thursday, I'll start with the same Facebook group, post another book, and run through all the groups over another ten-day period. I don't suggest doing more than two books as it will be very time consuming. For my purposes, of the two books I post, one is a 'first of a series' book.

I allot an hour a day for social media and do so usually in the morning and in the evening.

I haven't found much success in Facebook advertising, but that's me, and I know others have. There are several gurus out there who can teach you how to do Facebook advertising, if you spend your money with them. Will it work? It is up to you to make it work, especially if you pay to learn how. Mark Dawson is a recognized expert and one of the leading Indie gurus who teaches Facebook advertising—Nick Stephenson has a system that uses Facebook as well.

BookBub is incredibly important to the Indie writer. You don't post to BookBub, and until you have reached more than a thousand followers, they will rarely grant you a BookBub feature, which can sell thousands of books in a day. BUT, even without a BookBub feature, BookBub advertising works if done properly. As a professional writer, it is up to you to learn how to do it properly.

I have attended workshops and seminars where David Gaughran, an Irish Indie Author and Indie advertising guru has spoken. He teaches an online course for BookBub advertising I have heard from others is excellent, and from having listened to him myself at author conferences.

Do not misunderstand me, I am not recommending you use the experts I wrote about above, but they are mentioned in case you want to seek more knowledge about advertising in your chosen profession. We will go into more depth with advertising in Chapter 14.

WEBSITES

We haven't yet touched on websites. Websites are important, very important. It is the one place where your reader can meet you and learn more about you than from the back of a book, or your Facebook or Amazon Author Pages.

Yes, a website is important. Again, unless you know how and what you're doing, invest the money with someone who can do it right—with one important caveat: don't just use anyone.

Just using any web designer is not your best option. Find a web designer who knows author websites, have your site built with the programming to allow you to make the updates and even do the SEO (Search Engine Optimization). I hired an excellent professional web designer and website programmer who built my site with WordPress so I can maintain, add to it, make changes as necessary, and I am able to do the SEO.

However you work out your website, the site, like the cover of your books, needs to look and work professionally. Make it user-friendly with easy to follow links and encouragement on the pages to go deeper. Make sure your newsletter sign-up is on the home page and most other pages and use graphics properly. Don't overdo it: it is important to make sure your book cover(s) stand out.

A word about selling books on your website. Many authors do this. I believe it is not a very professional way of presenting yourself as a professional writer/author. I'm unaware of any best-selling authors selling books directly from their websites. Many non-fiction authors do sell on websites that appear as their own, but these are one, two, or three-page promotional sales sites, while some non-fiction authors do sell on their sites. This would be a decision you must make.

By posting your books with a buy button leading to Amazon, or iBooks, or others is not directly selling books on your website; rather, it is allowing your readers (or potential readers) to purchase your book from their regular bookstore, be it online or from a brick and mortar bookstore. In the beginning, if you only have the single book, don't let it phase you. Create a blog page and begin blogging. Blogging is another way to do some extra early marketing and, later on, reinforce your book with added pushes from the blog.

Let's recap. Early marketing is a strategy to help you sell books out-of-the-gate, so to speak. Your name starts to become familiar to the people in the book groups on Facebook and Goodreads, possibly a few Yahoo groups, and some Google groups as well.

Your website will now start to be your online office. Using your website, you proudly count down the days to book launch, and talk about subjects surrounding the book.

And as you approach the launch point, you begin to build your posts stronger by using early reviews from your beta readers and the other reviewers to whom you've sent ARCs

That's it for early marketing. Make good use of social media and it will be good to you!

CHAPTER 13
STEP 13
Reviewers and Reviews

Of course, I heard your question, you're shouting! *So, how do I get reviews before the book is out?*

Actually, it isn't all that hard. You've downloaded your ARC in a Mobi file. If you've signed on to either Draft2Digital or Smashwords, you also have an ePub and a PDF file. The ePub and Mobi files are the most important.

Before we get into that, there are some ground rules. Yes, I know, there are always rules ... Amazon will <u>not accept a review</u> of a book unless one of two criteria are met.

1. The person reviewing has purchased either an eBook or a Print book <u>directly from Amazon.</u>
2. The reviewer uses one of the following terms:
   a. "I received this ARC in exchange for an honest review."
   b. "I received this book as a gift from a friend."
   c. "I received a free copy of this book in exchange for doing an honest review."
   d. "I am a reviewer and received this ARC in exchange for an honest review."

The other retail sites also watch out for reviews and require similar adherence to the review rules. The smartest thing you can do is to make sure your early reviewers are up front and honest. OH ... and don't write your own review.

Now that we have the rules laid out, how do you find reviewers? One of the best ways, is to ask for a review. Look to book review websites such as Big Al's, that have a strong Internet presence. It is not easy to get reviewed on Big Al's Books & Pals [http://booksandpals.blogspot.com/], but you should try it anyway. To be honest, anyone who decides to write for a living, must, by necessity, be an optimist; therefore, you keep on trying until you succeed!

There are a lot of book review websites offering to review your book for a fee. You are a pro, you don't need a paid review, it can come back to bite you. Look for reviewers on book blogs, on websites. If you are unpublished, you can become an associate member of a writer's association. Local chapter members usually have critique groups, and they do write reviews too. Two examples are Romance Writers of America (RWA), and the Mystery Writers of America. The RWA has local chapters everywhere in our country so if you are a romance writer, join, today! The Mystery Writers of America also has chapters spread throughout the U.S.

Speaking from experience, the writer members all bend over backwards to help new writers get a leg up. And even the stodgy old writer's organizations refusing entry to anyone until they reached a set amount of Traditionally published books (from 1-3) have eased their restrictions. Recently these organizations have decided to allow Indie published writers to join after achieving a certain amount of sales, usually around five thousand dollars in a single year. The Mystery Writers of America, The Science Fiction and Fantasy Writers of America, and the Author's Guild now recognize Indie Authors who reach a certain point in their book sales.

ALLi, the Alliance for Independently Published Authors is an organization built by and for Indie writers. It is a place where you can find kinship with other Indie writers, and find a few of the pros who will read and review your works.

While I digressed about organization, it was for a reason. There will be more about professional organizations in Chapter 17. **Peers help peers:** asking for reviews is the most important and direct way of getting reviews. You can e-mail the various book review websites, not the book review service sites, but the book reviewers' websites, blog sites, or book podcasts.

Bloggers and Podcasters are always looking for a good book to review and talk about. But be forewarned, your book had best be professionally ready: formatted, edited, with solid plot and characterizations, and a great cover if it's fiction. The same goes for non-fiction, but exchange plot and characterizations, for facts and information.

There are a plethora of services offering to review your book for a fee. Even Kirkus charges, and their charges are substantial. In general, I suggest staying away from paid reviews, they never seem to be what you need. An additional warning about Kirkus. After giving them several hundred dollars for a review, there is no guarantee it will be a beneficial review. The Kirkus reviewers do not just give good reviews because you've paid them. They review a book and give their experienced opinion. They have an extremely high reputation to uphold. If the book isn't up to their standards, they will let the world know.

However, there are always exceptions to the rules and there are services you pay to find reviewers for you, but you do not pay their reviewers. These services bring in readers, who are subscribers to the service, and who read because they love to read, and they get free books. Once again, they must use the correct language or what they review will not get posted. They must state they have received the book for free in an exchange for a review.

There are also a few services that require you to send them a gift certificate so they can purchase the book from Amazon. With these review companies, you need to really research them to make certain they are truly legitimate.

One more word of caution: do your best to make sure the reviewer reads your genre; and understand, some of these reviewers may never post a review because a few do this just to get the books.

Why do I need a lot of reviews? A few good ones should do the job.

Not really. Reviews play several important roles in your book's life and salability: Readers take reviews to heart when deciding on what to read next; and, promotional websites, which can be your lifeblood for sales require a certain amount of reviews.

What is needed to get started with the promotion sites is usually a minimum of five reviews, but preferably ten. At the ten review point you can avail yourself of many of the better promotional services. But be warned, they usually require the reviews to have an average of at least 4.0 on a five-star scale.

A few paragraphs ago, I mentioned asking for a review. Besides the review services, the authors' associations, and people you know, there are those writers whom you admire. What about them? They had to do what you are doing now to get where they are. Ask them as well. You will be surprised by what can happen if your letter or e-mail is a well written request.

A personal anecdote. For those of you who are Sci-Fi people, I started reading Andre Norton when I was eleven. I thought he was a great writer. A few years into reading Andre Norton's Sci-Fi and Fantasy books, I learned Andre Norton was a woman. I was surprised, yet strangely pleased that I had learned her deep secret.

Well, twenty years later, I figured out a way to get her address and sent her a letter asking if she would read my fantasy novel. Two weeks later her letter arrived, , (yes, snail-mail: eMail was not yet in the public venue) and she did indeed say yes. She gave me a great cover quote, which I still use today.

Andre and I continued corresponding, and she mentored me in my writing. Andre Norton, for those not familiar with her, was the first woman to be named a Grand Master of Science Fiction by the Science Fiction and Fantasy Writers of America, the first woman to be Gandalf Grand Master of Fantasy, and the first woman to be inducted by the Science Fiction and Fantasy Hall of Fame.

Andre Norton helped my novel, *Queen of Knights* do well.

Now, in the interest of full disclosure, I have done this several times. I've had some successes, and some failures, but if you really are a professional writer, failure within the writing environment should be nothing more to you than fuel for success—and occasionally a little scotch, tequila, or bourbon to help swallow the review pill.

So, don't just sit on your butt, act! As an Independent writer/author, the only person you can blame for any lack of success, is yourself.

And please be a professional when it comes to reviews. If someone posts a bad review on one of the websites, don't get angry and respond ... do as the Beatles say, *Let It Be.* Try to remember as well, if you don't have any bad reviews, you're not doing your job either. Great books, best-selling books, and literarily magnificent books all get bad reviews.

"What good is a bad review?" you ask. Because of the amount of poorly written books published by vanity writers, as well as unprofessional Indie writers, people have become wary of reviews. I have been told by readers, time and again, when they see nothing but great reviews on books, they tend to shy away. If everyone says it's a great book, then the thinking is that most of the reviews are bought reviews or friend and family reviews.

If you've ever noticed, Amazon lists the best review and the worst review on the book's review page. Why? To give the potential purchaser a spectrum of other readers' opinions, not just the good ones. A high number of five stars with a good number of four-star reviews, and a few two- and three-star reviews set a sense of honesty to the overall rating.

To give you a further look into how reviews work, I saw one review, a one-star review. Was the book that bad? I don't know, but I do know this person blasted the cover because it didn't reflect what he thought it should. There was not one mention of the writing, the story or anything other than the cover. So, keep in mind you can never know what irks or pleases someone.

Oh, there is one more method of getting reviews—from the reader. Yes, you want everyone who reads your book to give it a review, correct? If that's the case, how? Simple! **On the page following the end of the book, put in a short paragraph, addressed to your reader, and ask for a review.**

Look, if you can ask a peer, a beta reader, even a reviewer to review your book, you most certainly can ASK YOUR READER for the same!

Here's one of my 'asks' on Amazon. (I use different review words/links for different retailers).

Dear Reader,

Thank you for taking the time to read *The Sokova Convention.* If you enjoyed this book, please consider telling your friends about it, and also consider posting a short review on Amazon, using the link below. Word of mouth and reviews are an author's best friends and every review and referral you give is appreciated. To post a review on Amazon, <u>please use this link.</u>

Thank you.

David

#

There is one more thing you can do, not just review-wise, but for the future. This is a step to take with any Indie book you publish; but, be warned—your book needs to be as near perfect as possible as to plot line, overall story, and overall quality of writing. It must be properly edited, and have a well designed cover. This option is the B.R.A.G. Medallion, and should be submitted the week your book is released, at the earliest.

The Indie B.R.A.G. Medallion
(https://www.bragmedallion.com)

The IndieBRAG mission is to discover talented Indie (self-published) authors and help them give their work the attention and recognition it deserves. Their primary focus is fiction across a wide range of genres; however, they selectively consider non-fiction books.

BRAGMedallion.com is a privately held organization bringing together a large group of readers, both individuals and members of book clubs, located throughout the United States and in ten other countries around the globe. **B.R.A.G.** is an acronym for *Book Readers Appreciation Group.*

The B.R.A.G. Medallion is an honor given to an outstanding work of Indie publishing.

*** In the print version of your book not published with Amazon, use the non-site specific phrases "go to the site where you purchased your book" or "To post a review, please use Google", or send them to your website.

CHAPTER 14
Step 14
Preparing the Advertising / Promo Schedule

(first and second quarters of the book's release)

Advertising and promotions can turn into a crazy amount of work, diverting your creativity, and eroding your writing time, so you need to think long and hard at how you want to advertise and promote your book(s).

You are an Indie writer, not a traditional writer and as I've said before, you don't have the same outlets as the traditional publishing houses. But wouldn't the *New York Times Review of Books* help give your book a running start? So, you'll need to find a smart yet cost-conservative way of advertising and promoting your book(s).

ADVERTISING

For the average writer, advertising usually falls into one of two categories: have a company or a consultant handle it and pay the fees, or do it yourself and take the time to study, learn, and create your advertising program. There are several people out there who make who make their living teaching you how to advertise on Facebook, Amazon, BookBub, because they are considered by many to be the top three places to advertise.

You should investigate each of the advertising arenas yourself before deciding on what you will do. You can hire a promotional agency or person, you can take the seminars and learn the in-depth lessons to accurately advertise, or you can study the advertising instructions on the sites.

In my opinion, the two best places to advertise are on BookBub (BookBub Ads) and on Amazon, using KDP advertising, followed closely by Facebook Advertising. You will need to thoroughly read all documentation to do this properly. The reason I place Facebook third, is because of the always shifting landscape, both social and political, these past few years.

The advantage to doing the seminars with professionals like David Gaughran, Mark Dawson, and Nick Stephenson (to name just a few), is because they are tried and true experts in their fields, they have developed workable programs to teach you their methodology, and they will help you. BUT, you will pay for it. The next question is, or course, will it pay you back in book sales?

The answer is not what you really want to hear. This is the publishing business, and no matter how hard the experts work to make everything seem absolutely logical, it is never truly so. One day the publishing world is wonderfully logical, the next day you feel like Alice who dove into the rabbit hole but missed and ended up with a concussion.

Advertising is a necessity for a starting writer, and a necessity for the experienced writer. The reason for the advertising is in how it brings you, the Indie writer, to the level of the traditional writer in the public's eye when they see your ads appearing on the same level as the traditional publishing houses. I'm not talking about full and half pages in magazines; rather, I'm talking about the ads on the Internet giants Amazon and BookBub and Facebook, and I'm sure you've seen them … the ones that are right under the book you've been searching for on Amazon., just off to the side or below the description on the page.

Just remember to watch them closely, after you've gotten the basic principles down, so you don't go overboard with your spending.

To get your book off to a good start, you should decide if you can do the advertising for yourself now, or wait until you learned enough to be confident in your ability to create and handle the advertising. Or, you start by using promotional websites to "push" your book. If it is your first, then you'll need to find several promo sites who promote with minimal reviews. There will be more of this in the chapter on your book's launch.

PROMOTIONAL SITES AND SERVICES

Briefly, your first promotional push, should be at full price, to introduce you and your book to the reading public. Hopefully within a few days, a review or two will come in. You can also do a discount as an introductory offer.

Several promotional sites such as The Fussy Librarian, Choosy Bookworm, Free Kindle Books and Tips, AuthorsXP, and eBook Betty offer new release features that do not have to be discounted to be promoted. AuthorsXP (Authors Cross Promotion) is a service where you can build your author's mailing list as well as do launch promotions.

Discounting can help the Indie author, if you do it right. There are a lot of authors out there who disagree that books should be discounted or given away free, but those authors usually have high sales and no need to induce readers. I believe you should do what helps you grow within the publishing industry, and if you discount, and gain readers (and fans) then there is nothing wrong with a promotional discount. But wait until book two is out before discounting book one unless it's a quick promotion.

Many Indie writers with a series have learned the use of discounting or giving away the first book to bring better sales for the entire series, but in the end, YOU are the publisher and YOU make the decision.

If your book is $2.99 or $3.99 (These are recommended eBook prices on Amazon) and you reduce it to $0.99 for the first week to ten days, you should garner enough sales to generate both reviews and interest in future books. Royalties are not something to be concerned with at this point. Getting a few dozen sales to generate customer reviews is more important. Don't worry about immediate sales, there is plenty of time.

Once you get moving and get reviews, then it's time to do other promotions, and those promotions should always have a boost from you on Twitter, Pinterest, and any social media you use. Your followers need to know if you are doing promos, so they can either pick up your books or tell others by retweets.

You should also create a newsletter. Try not to be annoying with it. Using a newsletter properly can bring you a new level of sales. However, with just one book available it requires a lower level of sales pitches with a greater level of socializing... What I mean by socializing is to introduce your readers to other writers who have good quality books, and are having a discount or free promotion special, which you can recommend to your readers.

If you send out a newsletter talking about more than just yourself, and introduce new writers and books to your readers, it will pay you back in sales as your publishing career grows, and you will also have created a base of peer writers who will happily repay you with mentions in their newsletters.

Newsletters are also the perfect way to build your reader base. And, remember, your newsletter is another way to personalize yourself to your readers, so don't forget to add some personal and/or family tidbits.

To have a successful promotion, you need the following to be done properly:

- **The Book Blurb**: A short description of your book to induce readers to purchase.
- **Keywords:** Make certain you have used the right keywords and phrases.
- **Cover**: A professionally created book cover that, like your blurb, helps to sell your book.
- Reviews.
- Online:
  - An Author website is highly recommended.
  - Amazon Author Page.
  - Goodreads Author Page (*suggested but optional*).
  - BookBub profile and book listing.

Remember your advantage ... your book does not have the short shelf life of a traditionally published book; but even the traditional authors are now learning to push their eBooks and print books after they're gone from the shelves. It's up to you to take your advanced advantage in promotions to keep your book(s) high in the rankings of each retail site.

**A list of vetted promotional sites is listed in the resources section.*

CHAPTER 15
STEP 15
The Launch

Getting ready for your book's release, you find the date you've set for your launch looming. You go over everything you've done, and you ask yourself, "What's next?"

The answer is preparing for your launch. As a "newbie" or a new Hybrid author, the launch process can appear daunting. If you've done everything you were supposed to, you're ready to prepare for the launch.

Your scheduled release date should be about sixty days prior to publishing—and don't forget, if you hit a glitch, you can always postpone the release for a few days or a few weeks.

What needs to be done to be ready in two months?

Your first decision is about where geographically, you want to launch, promote, and sell your book. There are four areas to look at: (1) Locally; (2) Nationally; (3) Internationally; and, (4) English-reading International countries. These can be done separately, or all together.

Unless you have a lot of money—think high five to low six figures—for advertising and promotion, you will be using the Internet. On the other hand, if you have that kind of money, you will be using a Public Relations service specializing in the publishing industry, or perhaps an Author's Virtual Assistant. So, for those of you (read that as us) who will be doing this yourself, there is a professional way, and there is a not-so-good way.

All I'll say about the 'not so good' way, is that it usually includes spamming all the social media one can get into with the total disregard for anyone else. I have no soft spot or middle ground for this, so I'll leave it here.

The scheduling for the overall release of your book should begin when you get the first edited copy. At this point, you want about ninety days to get everything ready. You should have an idea of when you are getting your cover, if you don't already have it.

Here's what I look at for a launch: this is not a written in cement way to publish your book, just my way of dotting the I's and crossing the T's. Remember, the thirty/sixty/ninety-day schedule does not mean on day ninety, you do all these things. Check out my schedule below, and work out your schedule through the first thirty says until you hit the sixty-day point, and then, of course do the same until publication day.

90 DAYS OUT

1. Completed edited manuscript.
2. Completed cover.
3. Formatted eBook manuscript.
4. Formatted print book manuscript (optional).
5. Pre-publishing upload for ARC copies.
6. ARC copies sent to beta readers.

60 DAYS OUT

7. Begin book launch tour set up.
8. ARC copies sent to book reviewers and book review blog sites and publications.
9. Continue with adding book tour blog sites.
10. Create newsletter (do not send out yet).
11. Post first blog. Use relevant content, mention the book ONCE!

30 DAYS OUT

12. Cover Reveal. (Many of the book tour blog sites will toss this in as a teaser.)
13. Send out more ARC copies to reviewers. (More is always good.)
14. Post second blog. (Again, mention the book once by using the cover reveal.)
15. Reread ARC copy, triple checking for any errors. This is your last chance before publication.

DAVID WIND

LAUNCH DAY !

Local Launch

A local launch is done within your hometown, city, and state. You will contact all the local media. Newspapers, radio stations, local print bloggers and video bloggers, libraries, and especially any bookstores you can get into. Bookstores are hard. One of the things you should have been doing, is making friends at YOUR local bookstores. You can even do that at a local Barnes & Noble, but you should understand if (and it usually goes this way) they adhere to their corporate rules, you have a very small chance of getting any help there, unless you also publish a print version through B & N, and then it's up to the local managers.

If you've done a print version (and if you are only publishing locally you should have a print version) your next step is around forty-five days prepublication. This is bookstore visit time, and it is when you bring an ARC copy of your book, signed, to the owner and/or manager. Do your homework first and have the inscription done before stepping into the store.

Independent books stores, just like you, are looking for ways to sell more books and stay both in business, and relevant. Indie book store owners are fiercely proud of what they do, and if you have one or two who feel your book meets all the professional standards of the traditional published books, and they have read and know your book meets all their criteria for selling in their store, they will be a strong advocate for you. But remember what you read earlier about print distributers, make certain you have a good print distributor like IngramSpark to supply books. Again, most booksellers will not order print books from Amazon, unless the books are returnable to the distributor, or the Indie author is willing to buy them back for what the bookstore paid.

Also, local doesn't just mean around the corner from where you live, local means a radius from where you live. I consider my entire state local. Once you have your local store behind you, you should be able to use that as a reference to the other bookstores to entice them to order your book. If you are publishing nationally and/or internationally, you should still visit your bookstore and follow the same procedure as local.

With a bookstore or two behind you, it's time to hit the news outlets—TV stations and newspapers. Either send ARC copies of your book, print is best, or bring them yourself if you believe you can get to someone there easier than through the mail or e-mail.

When you send out queries to your local newspapers and magazines, do not forget radio and television. Local stations are always looking for something new, something different. Authors are a good filling for their appetite. Cable shows are great places as well, especially if the shows are book related, or if their subjects are related to the plot of your book, the location, or the genre of book.

For most professional writers, a library is a solid marketing place. Talk to your librarian, introduce yourself as the author of a book, and see if they have any programs where you could appear and talk on the subject of your book. Most small libraries have free programs and many a library goer is a want-to-be writer who will come to these programs to learn as well as those people who look for free and entertaining programs. This is yet another means for gaining potential readers. Libraries will also buy your eBook so it can be available to their patrons.

Like the opening of a small business, a book launch is introducing your product to your local area and offering an invitation to meet you and then buy your book. Success locally will help you to succeed on a larger scale as well.

The National/International Launch Tour

There are two basic ways to do a book launch tour: With a full launch service; or on your own. You're an Indie author, and you should get used to doing things on your own. Yet, *on your own* doesn't necessarily mean you do everything yourself; it means you find and locate the experienced people and professional consultants/services you need for a specific segment of the launch and determine if you can afford them or not. If the answer is no, then you start learning.

The international book tour is the same as the English language country tour. People all over the world read books in English, and by concentrating on English language blog sites, you will reach those people. The only difference is that in the pure international tour, you will seek out blogs in the country's native language.

Understanding how to do these things is a long term benefit, because once you've done something, you know more than just how to do it, you know what it takes: the time it consumes; the contacts needed; and, when you investigate a service or consultant, you have gained enough experience and insight to know if they can do the job as well as or better than you.

Some author service companies are expensive, others less costly. For example, one of the reputable and less costly services, beyonddeflit.com has a five-day blog tour for under a hundred dollars. Also check out Reedsy, for additional launch advice.

When undertaking a launch tour yourself, you are the one making the arrangements, you have the control of deciding which blogs to visit, which social media avenues will work best, and how fast or slow to go. Yes, it takes time. Hiring a service to do this takes money, and time, but not as much time as the DIY option.

When I started out, I hired a book launch service, which was an interesting experience. But I also learned the steps in doing a launch, so I am able to do my own when I choose to do so.

Whether you do it yourself, or not, you still need to keep your finger on the pulse of each day's events. A good book launch tour will last ten days to two weeks with the heaviest concentration in the first week. During the launch period, you should visit at least one book blogger a day. You can do more, but you'll need to think about your time. If the blog is successful, it means their subscribers are interested and will make comments. When they do, the ABSOLUTE BEST THING POSSIBLE is for you to respond in a timely manner, with a personal comment. Timely doesn't mean five or six hours later, or even the next day, within an hour or two would be my recommendation.

Please look at your book launch in the same way you want to present yourself as a professional writer. Respond properly and don't use off-handed comments. You have a chance to build an audience, to make a reader yours, and to sell books. When you are on a virtual book tour, you do this one reader at a time, just the way you would if it was a physical tour and you were sitting in a bookstore.

If a reader likes your writing after reading your book, and buys your next book, you can be confident they will tell their friends about this wonderful new author.

Your next consideration is to understand there is an entire industry of "launch" bloggers and promotional sites spread throughout the world, not just locally or nationally. They are everywhere; and *everywhere* equals sales *everywhere*.

Don't forget about Internet Radio Shows—podcasts. Being interviewed on a book podcast can be very helpful to your book sales, but you need to be cool, calm, and collected, informative, eager yet controlled, and able to respond to questions with ease. This is no different than being interviewed on a radio talk show, or local and network television shows.

The local, national, and international book tours should be supplemented by the use of promotional sites like the ones below, which make provisions for new books.

- The Fussy Librarian:
  https://www.thefussylibrarian.com/advertising
- Choosy Bookworm:
  https://www.choosybookworm.com/promote-your-ebooks/
- Free Kindle Books & Tips:
  https://fkbt.com/for-authors/
- eBook Betty:
  https://ebookbetty.com/authors/
- Authors Cross Promotion/AuthorsXP:
  https://authorsxp.com)

Consider your book launch to be the foundation you are constructing for your ongoing career by using marketing, advertising, and blogs. Handle this correctly, build on the initial launch, and your books will sell.

But it is just the foundation, and without continued concentration on your promos and advertising, you will not grow the way you should. So, while your book is being prepared for publishing by going through all the processes needed, take an hour or two a day to study the various advertising sites, use their tutorials and FAQs, and check out online websites that help explain how to do the advertising and marketing.

That's it for the basics of launching your book.

CHAPTER 16
Step 16
Marketing, Indie Style

>Launch Release Marketing
>Social Media Marketing
>Ongoing Marketing
>Promotions
>Advertising
Launch Release Marketing

<<GROAN>> "I thought the launch release people, or the blog tour bloggers handle that stuff?" They do, and it is not what we're going to discuss.

Launch release marketing is exactly what it sounds like. Marketing set around the launch. This is slightly different than regular social media advertising, as it is more concentrated and time consuming on your end.

Facebook, Twitter, and all your other social media accounts should be used. Yes, the bloggers, reviewers and interviewers will do their own PR work, but they'll give you what every person appearing on their blogs gets—unless we are talking Stephen King, James Paterson, J. K. Rowling level best-sellers. They give the best marketing they can to drive readers to their site. It is the blogger who they read and listen to for literary advice. After all, they are the blogger's readers and they don't know you … at least not yet.

In reality, launch marketing means early in the morning tweets and posts, mid-morning, lunch time. Seriously, how many people do you know who do Facebook with their lunch? Probably a lot. Don't forget mid-afternoon, just before dinner, and of course, don't go to bed without … yeah, you got it.

A few days before the launch, I do social media marketing the way I described above, usually pointing the people to my website, with the full launch schedule, or to Facebook with the full launch schedule in the EVENTS section.

The first day of the launch tour is the first day your blog-specific posts and tweets, sending your followers to those bloggers. In between, you must visit the blog and see the responses. DO NOT BE DISAPPOINTED if there is not a lot of action. Book blogs are revisited quite often by their individual subscribers: most readers work, so there may not be much movement during the day, although with romance readers the daytime stats are often different.

Once again, remember you are the professional writer. You need to respond in that manner. Often, people will ask advice on books and on writing and publishing. Don't try to be a know-everything-person. Your responses need to stand up to research, and if you don't know the correct answer to the question, or do not know if what you are going to say is in fact correct, either look it up before responding, or be honest and say you are not sure, and will find out and get back to the reader.

I can tell you from experience, responding properly and professionally will give you a new reader for your launch book, and probably a fan as well.

Social Media Marketing

I think we all know, in general, the purpose for which writers use social media marketing. The real question is how to do it without being annoying, repetitive, and non-spammy! Ah, SPAM! The curse word of the Internet.

If you do a lot of posting on Facebook, you might or might not have been sent to Facebook jail. For those who have not yet had the pleasure, Facebook jail is when the folks (and the bots) behind the scenes (and screens) decide you are spamming and lock you out.

Facebook jail is the bane of the author who over-posts. And it can hurt because it can last for a day, a week, or a month. It can even get you banned from Facebook. So, how do you not go to jail? By (1) Being a professional; (2) Being a non-spammer; and, (3) By adding a bit of conversation in your heavier and oft repeated copy and paste marketing posts. Yes, copy and paste because you don't want to spend a day posting; you want to write, I would hope.

And if you do get sent, 'up the river' as the Mafioso say, start pleading to the eyes behind the screens. There are ways to not go to jail, but you need to keep rules 1, 2, and 3, uppermost in your mind. Copy and paste away, but do not hit 'Post' until you put some words in yourself. Like they say, different keystrokes show a human, the same copy and paste post shows a spammer to the Facebook police.

Once a book is launched, I run a twice a day posting routine on Facebook, and then run a three to four tweet posting routine on Twitter. I use either Tweet Deck or Hootsuite so I can schedule the tweets for anywhere up to a week ahead. The same can be done with Instagram, if you are a good Instagram user, and with Pinterest as well. While I don't use Pinterest, I know a lot of writers and authors who use it and swear by it. A lot of books get sold via Pinterest.

The real truth about social media is simple. You need to find what works best for you. For me, Facebook is one of my better sources. Between posting in book groups, posting on my own page, and doing occasional advertising, I sell books!

Ongoing Marketing

Ongoing marketing is exactly what it sounds like. Once you start, you just keep-on-keeping-on, as they say. If you stop, you will see sales drop as you stop enticing new readers to your books. I learned the hard way, once you take a significant break from social media marketing, it takes almost the same amount of effort to regain your momentum. My advice is simple: take your breaks after you set up whichever social media outlets you can do with advanced scheduling.

Facebook posts can be done with less frequency, but there is rarely any place in the world you can't post from. And taking fifteen minutes a day shouldn't be a hardship.

As I mentioned earlier, there is one more extremely important area of ongoing marketing: Newsletters. Your newsletter, depending on whether you want to do a monthly, bi-monthly quarterly or semi-annual newsletter, should be a constant.

By building up your newsletter subscribers, you are building a group of readers and fans who will most likely buy your books, post reviews, and tell their friends about you. A newsletter is one of the best ongoing marketing avenues for you and your writing. Don't be remiss, set up a newsletter. There are many e-mail services available, such as MailChimp and Constant Contacts, and most do not charge until you hit a thousand or two thousand subscribers.

One important service option for newsletters is list-building services such as Authors Cross Promotion (AXP). The AXP service is an example of one of many such services that will help you gain subscribers. But as I continue to say, be careful and research wisely before committing to anyone.

Promotions

Promotions are the lifeblood of an Indie author for they can pump new life into your sales. There are several types of promotions, depending on whether you are exclusive to Amazon, or you are distributed wide.

The two most relevant promotions are the FREE and the $0.99 cent promotions.

"FREE? Who the hell gives away their books for free?" you ask.

"I do," I reply.

Truthfully, I dislike giving away books I've spent so much time and effort creating, but I've learned how powerful a marketing tool it is when used to introduce yourself to readers.

Free doesn't necessarily mean no return of sales. Putting your book out on a free promotion can sell hundreds, and sometimes thousands of copies of your book. Yes, you did not mis-read, I said free books make money.

If you set up a free promotion properly, and use three to five promo sites, you can give away anywhere from hundreds to thousands of copies of the book on promotion. If you have more than one book available, then this turns into hundreds and thousands of leads for selling your other book(s). If it is your only book, a one-day giveaway has the potential to sell hundreds of books over the next several days.

The first time I did a free promo, I had more than two thousand books downloaded. Over the next eight days, I sold hundreds of copies of two other books, and close to a hundred copies of the book that had been free.

It isn't easy to loan out your eBook or get around the constraints of eBook distribution policies. As anyone who has tried knows, there are ways, but those ways are governed by the sellers, like Amazon. So, when enough people start reviewing and praising your book (that they downloaded for free) and your reviews begin to climb, your book will sell.

When I run free promotions, I have found it rare to not cover my expenses. I usually sell more than enough books to cover costs and make a profit on the sales. Sometimes the profit is marginal, but in the long run, every time a reader who has downloaded a free book, buys another of my books, it reaffirms the promotional process and the time spent on it, and brings in a stream of royalties.

There are hundreds, if not thousands of promotional sites. You need to do your homework and check out what others recommend as the best sites. Use them and chart the results. After running the promos, I'm confident you'll have found a group of promo sites that work for you. I'm putting a short list of sites in the resource section of this handbook, but you still need to do your homework to discover which ones work best for you.

The two main sites for you to shoot for are Amazon's KDP Select promotions, and BookBub. However, you can only use KDP Select if your book is exclusive to Amazon.

We'll start with BookBub, which is possibly the single most important promotional book site on the Internet. There is no charge to set up an account on BookBub (https://partners.bookbub.com) Make sure to fill out all the information, including your full Bio, and begin to 'collect' followers. Followers are your readers and other authors who like your writing. You should be collecting followers for BookBub, for your Amazon page, and for Twitter and Facebook.

Followers are the lifeblood of your marketing, the beating hearts of your readers and your fans. You need them to spread the word, and you need them to look at you as a professional writer, not someone who is throwing words on a page to make a few bucks—which is where your social media accounts come in to show the world your focus is on your writing.

BookBub is possibly the most influential of the promotional websites with millions—yes, millions—of subscribers, which gives them an amazing reach. It is also extremely difficult to be selected for a featured deal. You should have all your books on BookBub, whether it is one or fifty. You should also recommend books to your followers, which earns you recognition in BookBub, and once you reach 1000 followers, you stand a better chance of getting a coveted BookBub Featured Deal, which depending on your genre, will reach hundreds of thousands of potential readers in a single day.

BookBub is also expensive. Expect to pay several hundred dollars for a free featured deal, and if you charge a discounted price for your book, expect to spend from five hundred to several thousand dollars for the privilege.

For those Amazon-exclusive authors, you have two major promotional avenues on Amazon. Either the Kindle Countdown, or the free days. Either work well, but even with Amazon's power, if no one knows you're doing these Amazon specials, it won't mean much, so you should also add two to three other promotional sites for every Amazon promotion you do. And if you can get a BookBub feature, your overall results will most likely, knock your socks off!

Other than BookBub and Amazon, there are several promo sites to help you sell your books. The Fussy Librarian, Choosy Bookworm, and Free Kindle Books & Tips are three low cost, high return promotional websites I have used for years.

Two exceptionally strong promo sites are Freebooksy and Bargain Booksy, which are run by Written Word Media, and are a higher cost option than the ones mentioned above. ENT—eReader News Today is an excellent promo site as well.

And don't forget, when you run a promotion, and set it up at least thirty days in advance, you need to make mention of it in your newsletter and/or your blog. If you do prize giveaways, such as Kindles or Gift Cards, make absolutely sure it's in your newsletter.

In summary, promotional websites for books are a strong and necessary way to reach readers without the heavy expenses of advertising. But it is incumbent upon you to remember that in order to succeed, you must do your research on each and every one of the promotional websites you consider using.

Advertising

Last but not least is advertising. But where? For those of us who do not have hundreds of thousands of dollars available to push our books in magazines like Publisher's Weekly, or advertise on radio or television, there are several lower priced outlets. Lower price doesn't always mean affordable, unless you are careful how you use your advertising dollars.

The most important advertising mediums are, Amazon, BookBub, Facebook, and at times, Google. I have used three of the four. They are all, to one degree or another, CPC (Cost per Click) advertising. The three of the four entities I mentioned above are all book-directed advertising mediums, targeting either readers directly, or targeting through readers of particular books, readers of specific authors, readers of specific genres, etc. Google offers you the ability to target readers, but in a slightly different way than the others. Google uses keywords and phrases to target the people interested in your book's subject. But you must make sure you select the proper keywords and phrases.

As I've mentioned throughout this handbook, there are experts in advertising waiting to help you and teach you, but it is up to you to check them out and decide if you want to use one, and then which one is best for you. Do your research!

CHAPTER 17
STEP 17
Professional Organizations

Professional organizations are important. They can help you on several levels, from craft to camaraderie, but you must qualify to get into a professional writer's organization. Most legitimate author and writer organizations have requirements pointing solidly to traditional publishing. While this is an issue, traditional organizations are slowly coming to understand the role of the independent writer/publisher within the publishing community and are slowly morphing into a more contemporary form of writers' representation.

The gold standards of professional writers' organizations are: The Author's Guild, Mystery Writers of America, Science Fiction and Fantasy Writers of America, Romance Writers of America, Novelist Inc., International Women's Writing Guild, Alliance of Independent Authors, Society of Children's Book Writers and Illustrators, and Sisters in Crime. However, these organizations are only some of the organizations available to writers, but it is important for you look each over and make certain it is for you.

There are far too many reasons to list here for joining one or more of these organizations. The importance of these organizations to a writer, is the manner in which it brings them into contact with other writers, and how it enables them to continue learning their professional craft from the masters of today's publishing world. Ongoing education in publishing and writing is another extremely important benefit of every single writers' organization.

Annual conferences and local chapter meetings of each of these organizations fill a void for writers who tend to be isolated in their work. Writers organizations bring together diverse people of diverse origins, ethnicity, and ideology who are all focused on one absolute: writing and making their writing better every time they sit down to create.

Many of the established writer/author organizations now have rules to admit Indie writers into their organization.

While they require a traditionally published author to have published one, two or more books and/or short stories, and meet a monetary threshold, they are now doing the same for Indie writers.

~#~

The Authors Guild: https://www.authorsguild.org/

The following is reprinted from the 'Who we are' page of the Authors Guild website as of June 2019:

*The Authors Guild is the nation's oldest and largest professional organization of writers. Since our founding, we have served as the collective voice of American authors, and have long supported the rich and diverse literary culture of our country. Our members include novelists in all genres and categories, nonfiction writers, journalists, historians, and poets. The Guild welcomes traditionally published authors as well as self-published, independent authors.

We are a guild in the traditional sense of the term—a group of artisans who have come together to create an association of authority and influence. We give authors—who belong to an often lonely profession—a sense of community and belonging, with opportunities for sharing, networking, and conviviality.

INDIE MEMBERSHIP

Indie/self-published authors who have earned at least $5,000 in the past eighteen months from their writing qualify for full membership.

The Author's Guild admits associate (unpublished) members.

~#~

The Mystery Writers of America [MWA]: https://mysterywriters.org/

The following is reprinted directly from the MWA website.

Mission Statement:

*Mystery Writers of America is the premier organization for mystery writers, professionals allied to the crime writing field, aspiring crime writers, and those who are devoted to the genre.

MWA is dedicated to promoting higher regard for crime writing and recognition and respect for those who write within the genre. We provide scholarships for writers, sponsor MWA Literacy programs, sponsor symposia and conferences, present the Edgar® Awards, and conduct other activities to further a better appreciation and higher regard for crime writing.

As an Indie/self-published author the following qualifying membership rule applies:

You have been self-published and have <u>earned a minimum of $5,000 in a single calendar year from</u> **approved** <u>mystery works</u> (novels, novellas, short stories, or suitable non-fiction titles, i.e., true crime, biographies of mystery authors, critical works about mysteries, their creators and characters, forensic works, or other nonfiction that is mystery or crime-related), either in print, electronically, or by way of an audio recording.

The MWA admits affiliate (unpublished) members.

~#~

Science Fiction & Fantasy Writers of America [SFWA]: https://www.sfwa.org

*The purpose of the Science Fiction and Fantasy Writers of America is to promote, advance, and support science fiction and fantasy writing in the United States and elsewhere, by educating and informing the general public and supporting and empowering science fiction and fantasy writers.

MEMBERSHIP

For full membership of an Indie writer, the SFWA requires a qualifying work of fiction to be a minimum 40,000 words and can verify minimum earnings of $3,000 in one year, and the earnings must have been after 2013.

The SFWA admits associate members: Due to the complexity of the SFWA's membership rules, please go to their page at http://www.sfwa.org/about/join-us/sfwa-membership-requirements/

~#~

Romance Writers of America [RWA]: https://www.rwa.org/

The RWA is the largest romance writers' organization in the world and is exclusively made up of romance authors of every romance genre. They have several different membership levels, but full membership is open to both published and unpublished writers. The other levels involve non-romance and non-writers.

~#~

Novelists Inc. [NINC]: https://ninc.com/

Novelist Inc., is an organization that (1) is exclusively for multi-published authors; and (2) is built around helping authors with the business of writing. They state: **NINC brings our many voices and talents together for one purpose—to help each of us manage our writing career throughout a lifetime.*

NINC has only one level of membership for writers—multi-published, either traditionally or Indie published.

NINC qualifying requirements for Indie writers are indie published work of at least 30,000 words with earnings of a minimum of $5000 over twelve consecutive months with an Indie title

~#~

Alliance of Independent Authors [ALLi]: https://www.allianceindependentauthors.org/

ALLi is an international independent author's organization. To join ALLi, you become eligible for author membership if you have self-published a full-length (50,000+ words) book for adults; or, a children's book of any length; or, a series of shorter books. A previously traditionally published book that you are preparing for Indie/self-publishing qualifies as well.

ALLi offers help to the independent writer in several ways, including vetted services partners from editorial through publishing. They have a newsletter dedicated to helping Indie/self-published authors.

Other notable organizations are:

~#~

International Women's Writing Guild
https://www.iwwg.org/

The Guild was founded in 1976. They state as a women's writing guild, they are culturally diverse. From the beginning, they've represented women from many backgrounds.

They wanted to make a place where all women writers feel welcome, inspired, and empowered by skills, resources, and mentoring.

Membership has only one restriction, you must be a woman who writes. Membership is open to <u>all women writers</u>, traditional or Indie, journalists, published or unpublished.

~#~

Sisters in Crime: https://www.sistersincrime.org/

Sisters in Crimes is an organization created to help women who write in the mystery genres. Their website says it best: *Sisters in Crime welcomes everyone who supports our mission to promote the ongoing advancement, recognition, and professional development of women crime writers.*

Sisters in Crime is thirty plus years in existence. It is not a women's only organization and welcomes all who write in the Mystery/Crime genre. Men who join Sisters in Crime, are called Brothers.

~#~

Society of Children's Book Writers and Illustrators:
https://www.scbwi.org

SCBWI has three levels of membership; Associate, Full, and PAL: Associates for unpublished writers and others; Full is for published writers both Traditional and Indie; and, PAL is for authors with at least one article published by traditional publishing houses.

There are many other organizations, most of these can be found on Google and Yahoo.

THE INDIE WRITER'S HANDBOOK

*Information directly from the Author's Guild website as of June 2019.

*Information directly from the Science Fiction & Fantasy Writers of America website, June 2019.

*Information directly from the Sisters in Crime website, Jun 2019.

*Information directly from the Society of Children's Book Writers and Illustrators website, June 2019.

*Used with permission of the Mystery Writers of America.

*Used with permission of Novelists, Inc.

CHAPTER 18
Resources and Author Services

This chapter will cover a small amount of the services and resources available to you as an Indie writer. Because there are so many services available to writers and authors, I am presenting a small group of those services and resources I have either used myself or have vetted through peer authors. I will leave you with one warning about these or any services: do your homework. Check out whomever you decide to use, before using that person or company. Whenever possible, ask other writers in your writers' groups, organizations, research online, or by speaking directly with others when seeking references.

~#~

FORMATTING

~#~

There are several types of formatting, from the basic manuscript formatting, through eBook file formatting and print book formatting. The formatters and services below have been vetted properly.

Beyond Def
https://www.beyonddeflit.com/formatting-services?
Beyond Def offers several services including formatting. The Beyond Def team is experienced and professional.
The Deliberate Page, Formatter Tamara Cribley: tamara@deliberatepage.com
The Deliberate Page and Tamara will format your book for either eBook, Print, or both, and have it returned to you in ePub and Mobi files, and a ready for print submission PDF.
My Book Designer
http://mybookdesigner.com/interior-book-design/

Debbie Stocco, of My Book Designer, offers book formatting of any type of book for paperback and hardback, digital pdfs, and eBooks (ePub and Mobi).

Interior book design is based on the complexity of the formatting (fiction being the least complex), the word count, and the number of pictures or graphics. A short fiction novel starts at $250 (as of June 2019).

Nicholas Rossis Nicholas@pearseus.com formats manuscripts for writers who publish exclusively on Amazon. Nicholas is a formatter of excellent repute.

Formatting help websites:
Alliance of Independent Authors
Amazon's KDP   (Kindle Direct Publishing)
Just Publishing Advice

EDITING

Pelican Proofing & PA Services: L.J. Redding, Editor.

After realizing the need for affordable services to small publishers and Indie authors, Lacie founded Pelican Proofing in 2013. Lacie's aim is to maintain the integrity of the author's voice, while producing a professional manuscript.

Lacie Redding has been my editor at Pelican Proofing since 2015 and has done an outstanding job of keeping my manuscripts clean, precise, and professionally edited and proofed. She works with her clients during and even after finishing your manuscript to make certain everything goes properly.

Contact: pelicanfreak@yahoo.com

Laurie Boris, Editor.

Editor Laurie Boris moved from traditional into the Indie publishing world as both an editor and author. Laurie is extremely talented and will work with you to edit and shape your manuscript.

I have known Laurie for many years and can attest to her abilities as an editor.

In her own words, she says, "I've been copyediting and proofreading for over twenty years. If you're polishing up your manuscript for self-publishing or for presentation to agents and publishers, let me help you go out looking your best. I offer reasonable rates priced by the job, free sample edits, and indie-friendly service. My main editing experience has been with fiction, but I've edited nonfiction as well. References available upon request."

Contact: https://laurieboris.com/contact_laurie/
Terese Ramin, Editor.

An experienced editor in both traditional publishing and Indie publishing, Terese Ramin has been writing and editing for over thirty years. Terese specializes in fiction, including romance and all of its sub-genres, mystery-suspense-thrillers, fantasy-paranormal, and literary fiction. Terese is highly recommend by Indie writers. Query Terese for prices for developmental editing, copyediting, and proofreading.

Contact: tereseramin@gmail.com

Victoria Landis, Editor

Victoria Landis conducts her editing work with Indie authors in several ways. Before committing herself to a writer's project, she requests they send her three pages from the middle of their manuscript. She'll read those, choose one or two, and make a sample edited page(s) for the prospective client. Some want all the proposed changes only to be in side comments, even the punctuation changes, and others would rather she make the changes on the document itself, but highlight them in red. Landis can estimate from these choices about how many hours it will take to edit the book and provide a fairly accurate expected cost.

How many sample edited pages are given to the client depend on what the client says they want—simple line editing or something more complex—as well as the author's writing level and the state of the manuscript. Line editing tends to go faster, so she can do more pages per hour. If the author hasn't yet attained a good level of self-editing ability, it will take longer.

Contact: http://www.victorialandis.com/contact.html

PROOFREADING:

Authors Cross Promotion: (AuthorsXP) Offers proofreading as one of its writer/author services.

Pelican Proofing:

https://www.facebook.com/PelicanProofing/

~#~

COVERS

~#~

Steven Novak, Graphic Cover Artist:

http://www.novakillustration.com/, novakillustrations@gmail.com

I have been working with Steven for several years, and he has done a dozen of my Indie covers. Here's what he says on his website: "I have worked with everyone from Indie authors looking to dip their toes in the market, to publishing houses both small and large. My job is always the same: give you a cover that will snag the attention of readers. My prices are affordable, my turnaround is fast, and best of all I love doing it."

I will attest to what Steven has said on his website; and, his prices are good, and his turn around time is excellent.

The Book Cover Designer: (TBCD)

https://thebookcoverdesigner.com

I have found their covers to be among the best *pre-made* covers. Here is a quote from TheBookCoverDesigner.com

Here at The Book Cover Designer we have more than 13,000 outstanding pre-made book covers priced between $50 and $500. Our variety of more than a hundred vendors includes up-and-coming, as well as veteran designers, who offer eBooks and full jacket covers in every possible genre. Each cover is sold only once, *which means that you won't end up having the same cover as some other author.*

Fiona Jayde: fiona@fionajaydemedia.com
Fiona Jade has a stellar reputation in the Indie industry as an exceptional cover artist. Check her website for further details.

~#~

Retailers/Aggregators/Distributors

~#~

We have pretty much covered the sales outlets in the book. This is a simple overview of the publishers.

RETAIL ONLINE STORES

Amazon.com – Kindle eBooks, Kindle Print Books: https://kdp.amazon.com
Amazon is the biggest book publisher in the world.
Amazon has two Kindle lines: eBooks and print books.
Kindle eBooks offers two types of publishing: Regular and KDP Select.
KDP Select offers a range of promo opportunities not given to general Kindle publishing. The promos include Kindle Countdowns and Kindle Free Days. To qualify for these promotions, your eBook must be exclusive to Amazon, and be sold by no other retailer, wholesaler, or aggregator anywhere in the world.
Royalties:
- 70% if the eBook price is between $2.99 and $9.99, under $2.99 it drops to 35%:
- over $9.99 from 70% to 35%.)

Apple.com - iBooks: https://www.apple.com/apple-books/
(This is a simple landing page).

Apple publishes eBooks on their iBook division of Apple. They have no restrictions about where else you can sell your book; however, if there is a SINGLE LINK MENTION of Amazon in your book, they will not publish it.

The only other restriction is, at this time, you must either use APPLE equipment to directly publish a book on Apple's iBooks, or go through the iCloud to submit with a PC.

Royalties:
- 70% Flat rate

Barnes & Noble – Nook Press:
https://press.barnesandnoble.com/self-publishing-services
Royalties:
- $0.99 - $2.98 -- 40%
- $2.99 - $199.99 -- 65%

I found no mention, any longer, of sales outside the U.S.

Kobo: https://www.kobo.com/us/en/p/writinglife
Kobo is a worldwide publisher, headquartered in Canada, with a huge reach into the world's markets outside the U.S., and makes for a good secondary source of foreign sales for U.S. authors.

Kobo publishes eBooks in the ePub format and accepts books without restrictions as to other sales venues.

Royalties:
- $2.98 and below: 45%
- $2.99 and above: 70%

AGGREGATORS

Draft2Digital: https://draft2digital
Draft 2 Digital is an all in one aggregator, distributing to all major online retailers and subscription services, and libraries. They also partner with print distributor Baker & Tayler. D2D's POD division will begin soon. Draft2Digital Distributes to Amazon, Apple Books, Barnes & Noble, Kobo, Playster, Scribd, Tolino,

24Symbols, OverDrive, Bibliotheca, Baker & Taylor, Google Play Book.

Smashwords: https://www.smashwords.com
Smashwords was the first aggregator and is the largest. Smashwords distributes to Apple Books, Barnes & Noble, Kobo, Enki, Blio, Inktera, Scribd, Tolino, Odilo, OverDrive, Bibliotheca, Baker & Taylor, Gardners, Smashwords Store, Smashwords Library Direct.

~#~

Beta Readers / Reviewer

~#~

BETA READERS
Authors Cross Promotion (AuthorsXP):
https://authorsxp.com/for-authors/find-beta-readers
For a small fee, AuthorsXP will find reviewers for your book. Please make certain you follow the instructions you receive when using this service.

GOODREADS:
https://www.goodreads.com/group/show/50920-beta-reader-group
Goodreads has a beta readers group where you may pick up one or two beta readers. Just be certain they read your genre.

Critique Match: https://critiquematch.com
This is a website set up for you to search out the perfect critique partner and/or Beta Reader.

~#~

REVIEWERS

~#~

When we spoke of reviews, I quite strongly stated you should not pay someone to review your book. I believe this completely;

however, there are services you pay, not to write reviews but to find people willing to read your book and write a review. This works, if you follow the rules governing reviews. But do remember, these people are not paid, so when they review a book, the review will be honest, and may not always be favorable.

Authors Cross Promotion: https://authorsxp.com/for-authors/elite

Authors Cross Promotion offers a paid service that brings your book to UNPAID readers, who will review your book. There are rules, so please follow them to be successful.

Broad Universe:
https://broaduniverse.org/learn-more/reach-book-reviewers/

This service puts your book on NetGalley, where hundreds of reviewers have the opportunity to review your book. There is a month by month charge for this.

Kirkus Reviews:
https://www.kirkusreviews.com/indie-reviews/

The oldest professional service available, and very expensive. They will review your book, but the results of the review are up to the individual reviewer, good, bad, or ugly. A good Kirkus review is worth a lot!

Big Al's Books & Pals: http://booksandpals.blogspot.com/

Big Al and his staff review books from around the world. The reviews from Big Al's are bitingly honest reviews. He and his staff are unflinching in their search for the best Indie books out there.

Reedsy: https://reedsy.com/discovery/submit

Reedsy's review service is an ethical review service. Please rea their requirements.

Use Google, Yahoo, or Bing to find more. Just be very, very, very, careful!

~#~

Marketing

~#~

AUTHORS CROSS PROMOTION (Authors XP)
https://authorsxp.com

Amy Vansant's AuthorsXP offers a half dozen types of marketing services. Amy, a successful author, and web designer started the AuthorsXP to help herself and her peers get through the daunting path of book marketing. What started small became much more. Amy and I are in a writers' group together, and I have watched AuthorsXP grow into a service that goes the extra mile to help authors, both newbies and veterans build their sales, their newsletters, and their fans.

In her own words, Amy says, "I created this site to help authors, particularly Indie authors, avoid all the pitfalls I had to slog through. New authors will find a quick way to solve a lot of their marketing and production problems, and more experienced authors will band together and GROW with our Mailing List Building events and Read & Review programs."

Bargain Booksy: https://www.bargainbooksy.com/sell-more-books-2/

Operated by Written Word Media, I find Bargain Booksy to be as powerful a marketing site for discounted book promotions as is Freebooksy for free promotion.

BookBub: https://partners.bookbub.com

BookBub is the current book marketing champion. With millions of subscribers, BookBub offers special features and a full advertising plan to their subscribers.

Choosy   Bookworm:
https://www.choosybookworm.com/promote-your-ebooks/

Choosy is another of those smaller (not small) marketing sites I use. Jay and his staff will bend over backwards to help you. They also have new release features. I use Choosy six to eight times a year.

Book Gorilla: https://www.bookgorilla.com/advertise
A strong marketing site. You will need to book this at least thirty to forty-five days in advance.

eBook Betty:
https://ebookbetty.com/author-submissions/
eBook Betty is another of my go-to sites. Inexpensive, it reaches enough subscribers to make it a worthwhile investment.

eBookSoda: http://www.ebooksoda.com/authors/
This is another of those smaller (not small) marketing sites I use with regularity.

Ereader News Today:
https://ereadernewstoday.com/bargain-and-free-book-submissions/v
ENT is a strong site for marketing to Amazon/Kindle readers and produces good results.

Facebook:
Log into your Facebook page, and begin to collect groups to post in.

Freebooksy: https://www.freebooksy.com/for-the-authors/
Operated by Written Word Media, I find Freebooksy to be a powerful marketing site when doing a free book promotion.

Free Kindle Books & Tips (FKBT):

https://fkbt.com/for-authors/

This marketing site is for free kindle books, and, offers a New Release promo, (free or not) on their Saturday newsletters. Michael also sends out newsletters filled with author tips to help you as you market your books. FKBT is another of my favorite promo sites.

The Fussy Librarian: https://thefussylibrarian.com

Not the biggest book marketing site around, but one of the steadiest. Jeffrey, the head librarian is knowledgeable and great to work with. This is one of my go-to marketing sites I use at least eight times a year. The Fussy Librarian does have special deals, so keep your eyes open for them.

Kindle Nation Daily (KND):
http://indie.kindlenationdaily.com/?post_type=produc
Good promo results plus an add-in with Book Gorilla.

Reign of Reads (primarily sci-fi/fantasy)
https://reignofreads.com/forauthors/
For Science Fiction and Thriller/Mystery. A good site.

The Kindle Book Review:
https://www.thekindlebookreview.net/advertising/
A good site for Amazon exclusive books.

In addition, the Alliance of Independent Authors (ALLi) has a book of recommended services they offer their members. I have not used any of their services; however, they have been vetted by the ALLi board.

There are hundreds of additional marketing websites. Be smart by being cautious in using any and all marketing websites.

~#~

Website Design

The Rhubarb Crew: lijaznak@gmail.com web design and marketing — Specializing in inbound marketing for small, mid-size businesses. Web design and development, graphic design, email marketing, social media consulting.

Istomedia Web Services: http://istomedia.com/ Istomedia has been developing websites and marketing on social media since 1995. It now specializes in author services and websites. eMail Nicholas@istomedia.com

~#~

EDUCATION

~#~

What I consider ongoing education comes in two forms: Author organizations and associations; and, online courses.

Your previous education, be it high school level, college level, or even post graduate level is not what I am discussing here. If you were an English Lit, an English major, or a Creative Writing major, good for you. You've got a step up, but don't take the step with tunnel vision, make certain you widen your scope.

Your education as a professional writer should be broadened with ongoing learning and understanding of your craft. One of the absolute best places to do this, is in conjunction with your author organizations.

There is one other aspect of being a member of a professional writer's organization and that is in meeting other writers, forming relationships, and being able to learn from each other on an ongoing and personal basis.

I know many writers who, having met other writers they can relate to, have formed writing groups, to help each other with the technicalities of writing, to be a critique group, and to support each other through the hard times and celebrate good times.

The following information is not all inclusive, but the tip of the iceberg in writing organizations and ongoing education through them.

~#~

The Authors Guild holds online seminars and in person seminars throughout the year. Most of these deal with professional issues to help you through the pitfalls and pratfalls of being a writer and making a living. http://www.authorsguild.org

~#~

Mystery Writers of America has almost a week of writing education during their annual EDGAR awards, which are the highest awards the Mystery Writers of America gives out. During that week the classes will help you through all the usual issues with writing, from plotting, to research, and beyond.

The MWA does something very interesting as well. The local chapters meet once a month, and has a social period, followed by a meal, either lunch or dinner, followed by a program featuring a speaker talking on a subject of which they are an expert.

Several MWA chapters have annual conferences that offer one, two, or three days of seminars and workshops. The Florida Chapter is known nationally for their annual Sleuthfest conference. https://mysterywriters.org/

~#~

Novelists, Inc., has an annual conference offering three plus days of educational seminars and workshops, as well as brining in a large amount of publishing professionals from both sides of the tracks. Traditional publishers are represented as well as Indie publishers. Draft2Digital, Smashwords, Kobo, Amazon, and Apple have been represented at past conferences, and after speaking with them this year, I have been told it will continue on in this way.

Many of the leading "gurus" of the Indie world come to Novelists' Inc, as well.

Novelist Inc., workshops and seminars go twelve hours a day, and the conference is well attended by both traditionally published authors and Indie published authors. https://ninc.com

~#~

Romance Writers of America like the MWA has a huge national conference. They have seminars running every day and evening, and their workshops are highly tilted toward education within the writing/publishing industry.

The RWA also has local chapters spread through the world, and these chapters are extremely active and do have their monthly meetings with guest lecturers/speakers keeping the education process moving forward for its members. https://www.rwa.org

~#~

Alliance of Independent Authors offers several educational venues:

ALLi offers a free online publishing course.

ALLi has a section called ADVICE. There is a blog that is educational, thought provoking, and should be tread by Indie writers with their morning e-mails. https://www.independent-authors.com/ These are a few of the educational opportunities available.

~#~

ONLINE COURSES:

There are always online courses to take, but which ones will benefit you? That's what you need to think about as you peruse the Internet. And please, do not take this listing as gospel. You're a writer, do your job, research!

GOTHAM WRITERS:
https://www.writingclasses.com/classes/online?gclid=CKT2Z qb2uICFYy1wAod9_gF7w

Gotham Writers offers online workshops, which are the same as their NYC in-class workshops.

MASTERCLASS: https://www.masterclass.com

Masterclass offers bestselling authors to teach you the craft.
REEDSY: https://blog.reedsy.com/learning/
Reedsy offers publishing courses and seminars.
WRITERS DIGEST UNIVERSITY:
https://www.writersonlineworkshops.com
Online writing classes from Writers Digest.

~#~

WRITING GROUPS

~#~

eNovel Authors at Work: https://enovelauthors.com/

This author group's website, founded by bestselling hybrid author Jackie Weger, offers a treasure trove of information for the Indie writer. Do not fail to visit their website! Membership qualification depends on your publishing history.

Quoted from their website:

We are dedicated to helping one another understand the challenges facing writers in the digital universe. Everything we discover finds its way into these pages to help authors and readers alike to navigate the universe of Indie publishing. Our Author pages are filled with an array of well-written and entertaining books across all genres, from sweet romance to edge-of-your-seat thrillers. We do not promote erotica or gratuitous violence. eNovel authors are scattered about our good Earth: USA, Canada, New Zealand, Australia, France, Greece, Scotland. Africa and the United Kingdom, but we all come together right here.

We are all about THE BOOK. We help each other to get our books noticed and expand our audiences. Indie Publishing is constantly changing. We do our best stay informed. Whether an author has published one book or ten, success requires diligence, dedication, and focus. We don't know all the answers, but we are learning who to ask, who to listen to, and how best to use the tools available to sell BOOKS in today's market. What worked last year or even last month may need tweaking. We've tried everything: Blogging, Interviews, Tweet Fests, Newsletter swaps,

Rafflecopters, Facebook events, Amazon Giveaways and promoting our titles free and discounted. Read the blogs to discover what works for us—or doesn't.

The Kboards https://www.kboards.com/
Kboards is a Kindle authors bulletin board. Use this, it will help find out about various services these writers have used, as well as what's happening Kindle-wise!

Facebook groups: Below are just a few. There are many more on Facebook.
Mystery & Thriller Writers Group
I Love My Authors Group
Writers' Group
The Writer's Circle
Writers Helping Writers
Naturally, the last option I have for you, for writing groups, is you. Find two to five more like-minded writers and form your own group. Believe me, this is not hard, and it is extremely valuable.

~#~

WRITING SOFTWARE

~#~

Scriveners at: https://www.literatureandlatte.com/
Snowflake Pro: https://www.advancedfictionwriting.com/
Microsoft Word: https://microsoft.com

~#~

Additional Resources

(in no particular order)

~#~

The Wise Ink Blog:
http://www.wiseinkblog.com/category/book-launch/   This blog has tips and how-to plan a tour.

Escape With Dollycas Book Tours:
http://www.escapewithdollycas.com/great-escapes-virtual-book-tours/ Dollycas is highly recommended by several authors I know.

BookBub: https://insights.bookbub.com/
(Their weekly blog)

BookBub: Book Launch Ideas
https://insights.bookbub.com/category/book-marketing-ideas/

Indies Unlimited: http://www.indiesunlimited.com/ This is an important website for Indie information. Make visiting this site part of your routine.

Jane Friedman: https://www.janefriedman.com. Jane Friedman has twenty years of experience in the publishing industry, with expertise in business strategy for authors and publishers. She's the co-founder of The Hot Sheet, the essential industry newsletter for authors, and has previously worked for F+W Media and the Virginia Quarterly Review.

Author consultant Mel Jolly of https://meljolly.com & authorRx.com:
"Keeping Creatives Out of the Loony Bin Since 2009"
An organizing genius, sign up for Mel's newsletter and learn tons about Indie writing, Organizing, Virtual Assistants, getting things done, and much more. https://authorrx.com/weekly-newsletter/

Author Consultants Tina Koenig (http://www.tinakoenig.com / 954-989-3338) is a literary consultant and publicist. She's worked with New York Times best-selling authors and indie authors. Tina's expertise is in building your author brand – from buying a domain name to building a website. If you're not a techie, Tina will take you through the process. She also schedules author tours and personal appearances. If you're working full-time, and need someone to help manage your writing career, Tina is who you call. She can be booked in 10 hour blocks of time or by the project.

Marketing Guru David Gaughran's Blog:
https://davidgaughran.com/blog/

Kindlepreneur – Dave Chesson, Online Book Marketing Classes: https://Kindlepreneur.com

The Book Designer:
https://www.thebookdesigner.com/

The Passive Voice:
http://www.thepassivevoice.com/. This is another important website for Indie and all publishing information. Make visiting this site part of your routine.

~#~

SOURCES:

~#~

The following sources have been used in this book.
WIKIPEDIA: https://www.wikipedia.org/
REEDSY: https://blog.reedsy.com/
GCFLearnFree: https://edu.gcfglobal.org
Google Search: https://google.com
Yahoo Search: https://yahoo.com
Bing Search: https://bing.com
NY Book Editors: https://nybookeditors.com/
Alli: https://www.allianceindependentauthors.org
MWA—Mystery Writers of America:http://mysterywriters.org/
RWA—Romance Writers of America https://www.rwa.org
SFWA—Science Fiction & Fantasy Writers of America:
https://www.sfwa.org

DAVID WIND

Authors Guild: https://www.authorsguild.org/
Novelists, Inc. https://ninc.com
The Book Cover Designer:
https://thebookcoverdesigner.com/

THE INDIE WRITER'S HANDBOOK

From the Author

Thank you for taking the time to read *The Indie Writer's Handbook*. If you found this book helpful to you, please consider telling your friends about it, and also consider posting a short review online. Word of mouth and reviews are an author's best friends and every review and referral you give is appreciated.

Thank you,
David

DAVID WIND

About the author

International award winning author David Wind, has published forty novels including Science Fiction, Mystery, and Suspense Thrillers. He lives and writes in Florida, where he and his wife Bonnie, share their home with their dog Alfie, a Moyan standard poodle. Moyan is French for middle—he is in between a standard and a miniature poodle.

A Hybrid Traditional and Independent Author, David left traditional publishing in 2008, to become an independently published writer . He published *Angels in Mourning*, his 'homage' to the old-time private detective books of the 50's and the 60's. He used to sneak them from his parents' night tables and read them as a young boy. *Angels* is a contemporary take on the old-style noir detective. *Angels in Mourning* won the Amazon.com Book of the Month Reader's Choice Award.

David's Contemporary Fiction novel, published in December of 2017, and based on the Harry Chapin Song, *A Better Place to Be*, was named a B.R.A.G. Medallion Honoree, signifying a book of the highest literary quality, and written by Independent writers; and rhe novel received the Bronze Award from Ireland's Drunken Druid International Literary Awards.

The first book of David's Sci-Fi Fantasy series *Tales of Nevaeh. Born to Magic*, an international Amazon genre Best Seller, and a Kindle Review of Books finalist for Fantasy Book of the year. The second and third books of the series, *The Dark Masters: Vol 2*, and *TRINITY: The Battle For Nevaeh, Vol. 3*, have both reached the Amazon Top 100 in its genre.

David's Fantasy, *Queen of Knights*, is a medieval fantasy based on actual events.

He wrote the medical thriller, *The Whistleblower's Daughter,* with Terese Ramin. The idea for this medical legal Thriller came shortly after the death of a close friend. David said, "I couldn't help but wonder about the medication...."

His suspense thrillers are *The Hyte Maneuver,* (a Literary guild alternate selection); *The Sokova Convention*; and, *The Morrisy Manifest. Out of The Shadows;* and, *Desperately Killing Suzanne,* are mystery suspense novels.

David's novels have been translated into eleven languages and published in fifteen countries.

David's Links

David's website:
http://www.davidwind.com
David's Amazon.com Author's Page:
http://amzn.to/1AKYcyR
David's Newsletter:
http://bit.ly/DMW-Newsletter
Facebook:
https://www.facebook.com/ authordavidwind
Goodreads Authors Page: http://bit.ly/1v1IE6B
BookBub Author Page:
https://www.bookbub.com/authors/david-wind
Twitter: @david_wind

DAVID WIND

Currently Available Novels by David Wind

Thrillers, Suspense, Mysteries
Desperately Killing Suzanne
Out of The Shadows
The Sokova Convention
The Morrisy Manifest
The Hyte Maneuver
The Whistleblowers Daughter
Angels in Mourning

Boxed Sets:
Cops Spies & PI'S
Tales of Nevaeh

Sci-Fi / Fantasy
Born to Magic , Tales of Nevaeh, Volume I
The Dark Masters, Tales of Nevaeh, Volume II
TRINITY, Tales of Nevaeh, Volume III
Prelude to Nevaeh: Roth's Story (A novella prequel)
Queen of Knights
Infinity's Doorway

Contemporary Fiction
A Better Place To Be: Based on the Harry Chapin Song

<><><>

For more information about David Wind, please visit http://www.davidwind.com.

For Information about special giveaways, free books (from myself and other authors), new releases and other news, please visit my website to sign up for my newsletter.

NOTES:

NOTES:

Made in the USA
Monee, IL
07 July 2026